SUMMER LINK

MATH *plus* READING

American Education Publishing™
An imprint of Carson-Dellosa Publishing LLC
Greensboro, North Carolina

American Education Publishing™
An imprint of Carson-Dellosa Publishing LLC
P.O. Box 35665
Greensboro, NC 27425 USA

ISBN 978-1-4838-0463-7

01-034147784

Table of Contents
by Section

Kindergarten Readiness Checklist 4
Summer Link Math 14
Summer Link Reading 119
Kindergarten Screening Guide 219

Summer Link Math
Table of Contents

Shapes 14–27
Big and Small 28–30
Patterns 31–32
Counting 1–5 33–57
Review Numbers 1–5 58–59
Counting 6–10 60–79
Review Numbers 1–10 80–82
Order and Sequence 83–86
Same, More, and Fewer 87–92
Numbers 93–94
Answer Key 95–103

Summer Link Reading
Table of Contents

Recommended Summer Reading 118

Colors 119–125

Shapes 126–131

Size 132–138

Comparisons 139–148

Letter Recognition 149–160

Writing Readiness 161–170

Beginning Consonants and Short Vowels 171–198

Answer Key 199–207

Developmental Skills for Kindergarten Success 208

Kindergarten Readiness Checklist

Young children grow quickly and develop skills at different rates. If they cannot do something this week, they may be able to do it a few weeks later.

While there is no perfect formula that determines when your preschooler is truly ready for kindergarten, you can use this general checklist to guide you as you prepare your child for school. Because each school varies, it is a good idea to contact your child's school in advance to find out it they have a checklist for you to use.

It is best to look at these skills as goals toward which to aim. They should be accomplished as much as possible through everyday routines or enjoyable activities that you have planned with your child.

Check the skills that your child has mastered. Then recheck every month to see what additional skills your child can accomplish easily.

If your child has acquired most of the skills on this checklist and will be at least five years old at the start of the summer before he or she starts kindergarten, he or she is probably ready for kindergarten. What teachers want to see on the first day of school are children who are healthy, mature, capable, and eager to learn.

KINDERGARTEN READINESS: Speech and Language Development

☐ Speaks in complete sentences.

☐ Speaks clearly enough to be understood by someone who does not know him or her well.

☐ Communicates well with peers.

☐ Can rhyme and recognizes rhyming sounds.

☐ Identify the beginning sound of some words.

☐ Identify some alphabet letters.

☐ Tells the meaning of some simple words, like "stop."

☐ Can recite ABC's and count to ten.

☐ Asks questions.

☐ Looks at pictures and can tell stories about them.

☐ Can answer questions about a short story.

☐ Repeats phrases said by an adult.

☐ Can communicate with both adults and peers.

KINDERGARTEN READINESS: Social Development

- ☐ Can be taken away from parents without being overly upset.

- ☐ Can spend extended periods of time away from parents.

- ☐ Explores and tries new things.

- ☐ Curious and motivated to learn.

- ☐ Puts away toys and helps with family chores.

- ☐ Meets visitors without shyness.

- ☐ Able to stay on task and work independently.

- ☐ Finishes tasks.

- ☐ Describes some basic emotions and feelings.

- ☐ Expresses feelings and needs.

- ☐ Recognizes authority.

- ☐ Gets along and plays cooperatively with other children.

- ☐ Can take care of own toilet needs independently.

- ☐ Feels good about self and talks easily.

- ☐ Dresses self and cares for own belongings.

- [ ] Waits his or her turn.

- [ ] Exhibits self-control.

- [ ] Seeks out interactive play with other children.

- [ ] Listens to stories without interrupting.

- [ ] Uses words rather than physical aggression to get what he or she wants.

- [ ] Understands that actions have both causes and effects.

- [ ] Beginning to share with others.

- [ ] Follows simple directions.

- [ ] Shows beginning of "empathy" skills.

- [ ] Knows parent's names, home address, and phone number.

- [ ] Can recite own first and last name.

- [ ] Says "please" and "thank you."

- [ ] Understands basic safety rules.
  Example: Don't talk or get in a car with a stranger. Look both ways before crossing the street.

- [ ] Aware of any food allergies he or she has.

- [ ] Can tell a story about a past event.

KINDERGARTEN READINESS: Motor Skill Development

☐ Runs, jumps, skips, hops, and gallops.

☐ Can bounce and catch a ball.

☐ Walks backward.

☐ Walks up and down stairs alternating feet.

☐ Can walk in a straight line.

☐ Uses hand-eye coordination.
    Example: Can jump on one foot, stand on one foot for 5-10 seconds, clap hands.

☐ Holds a pencil or crayon correctly.

☐ Holds scissors and cuts correctly.

☐ Can use scissors and glue to cut and paste.

☐ Can trace basic shapes.

☐ Builds with construction toys and blocks.

☐ Draws and colors beyond simple scribbles.

☐ Can put a 10 to 12 piece puzzle together.

☐ Can button, zip up zippers, or snap clothing.

☐ Ties own shoes.

KINDERGARTEN READINESS: Academic and General Knowledge

- ☐ Can write full name and recite address.

- ☐ Recognizes own first name in writing.

- ☐ Knows basic shapes.

- ☐ Knows colors.

- ☐ Knows relative sizes.
     Example: *big–small* or *small–smaller–smallest*

- ☐ Recognizes and completes patterns.

- ☐ Knows body parts, such as nose, ear, elbow.

- ☐ Can match similar objects and explain why they are alike.

- ☐ Can count to twenty.

- ☐ Knows ABC's and can recognize and write most letters.

- ☐ Can memorize things that have been read to him repeatedly.
     Example: pretends to read a favorite story.

- ☐ Understands that print carries a message.

- ☐ Uses left to right progression.

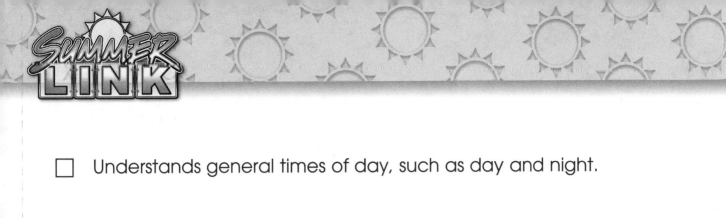

☐ Understands general times of day, such as day and night.

☐ Knows own age and birthday.

☐ Understands position and spatial concepts, such as *up*, *down*, *full*, *empty*.

☐ Identifies simple opposites.

☐ Can sort items by color, shape, and size.

This page intentionally left blank.

13

Shapes

Directions: Trace the **circles**.

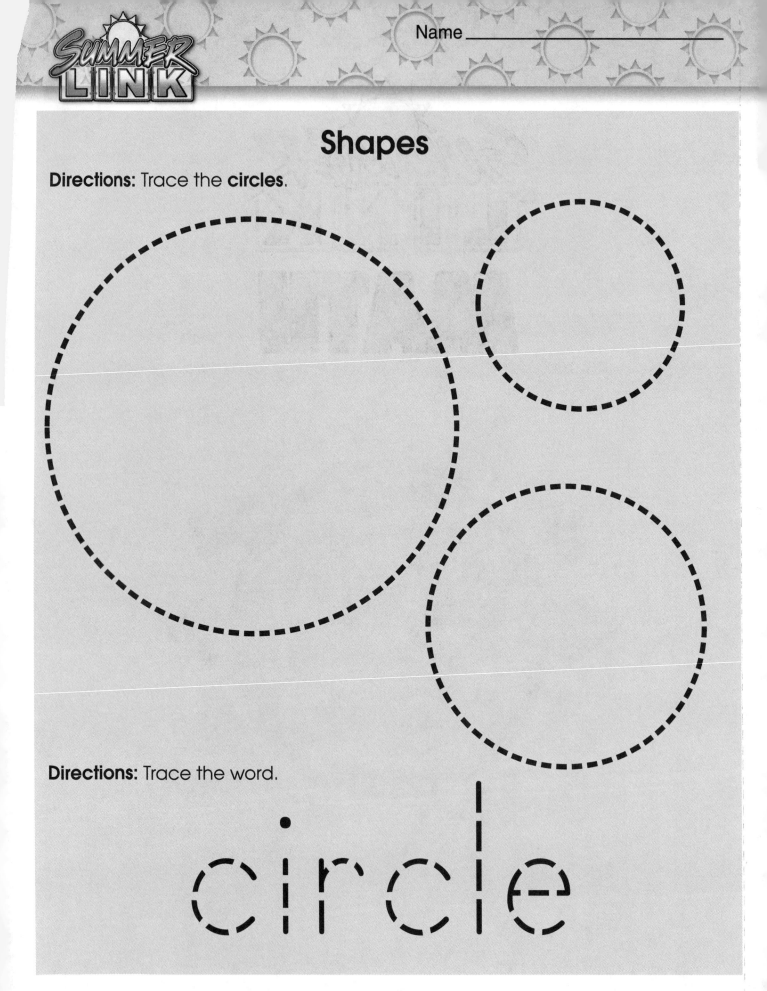

Directions: Trace the word.

circle

Shapes

Directions: This picture has **circles** in it. Trace the circles.

Shapes

Directions: Trace the **squares**.

Directions: Trace the word.

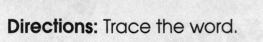

square

Shapes

Directions: This picture has **squares** in it. Trace the squares.

17

Shapes

Directions: Trace the **triangles**.

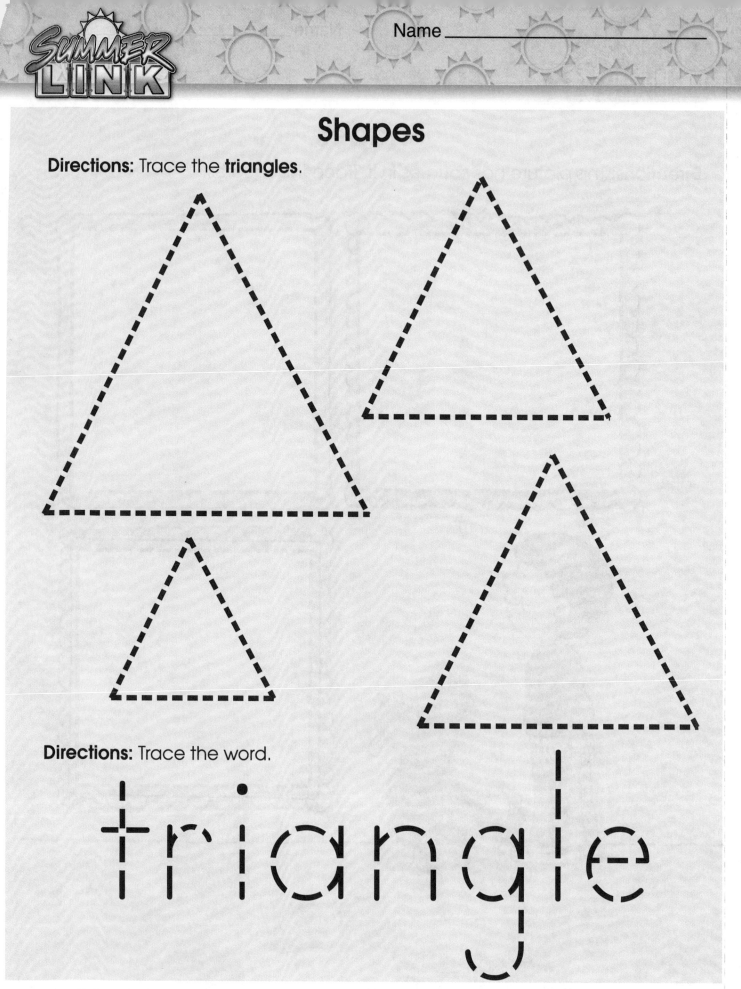

Directions: Trace the word.

triangle

Shapes

Directions: This picture has **triangles** in it. Trace the triangles.

Shapes

Directions: Trace the **rectangles**.

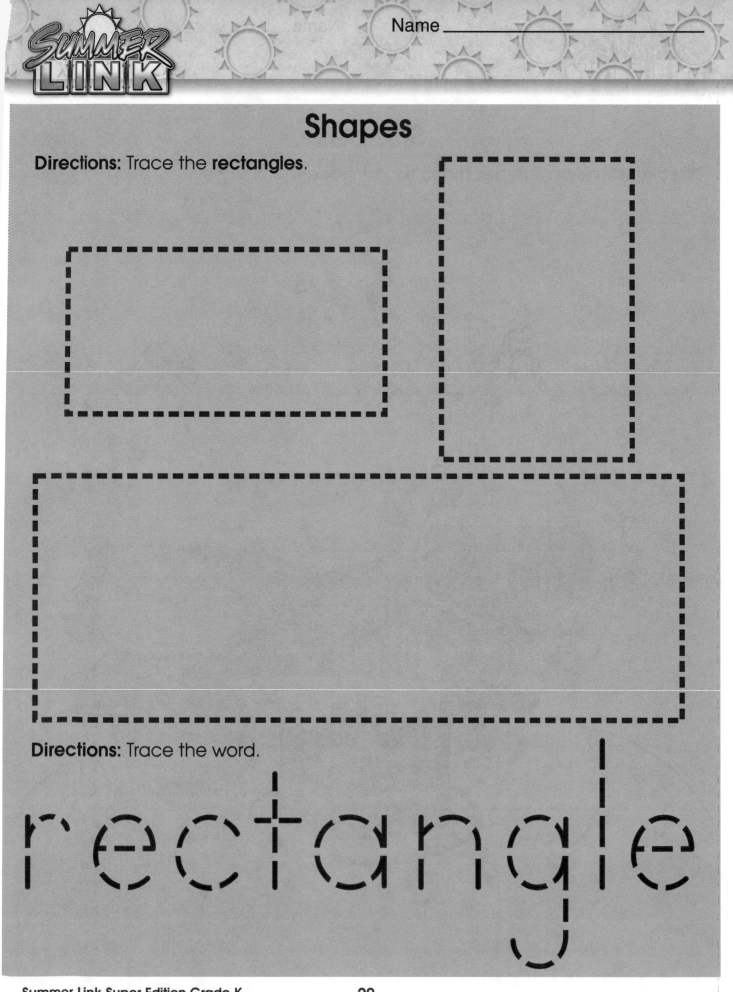

Directions: Trace the word.

rectangle

Shapes

Directions: This picture has **rectangles** in it. Trace the rectangles.

Shapes

Directions: Trace the **ovals**.

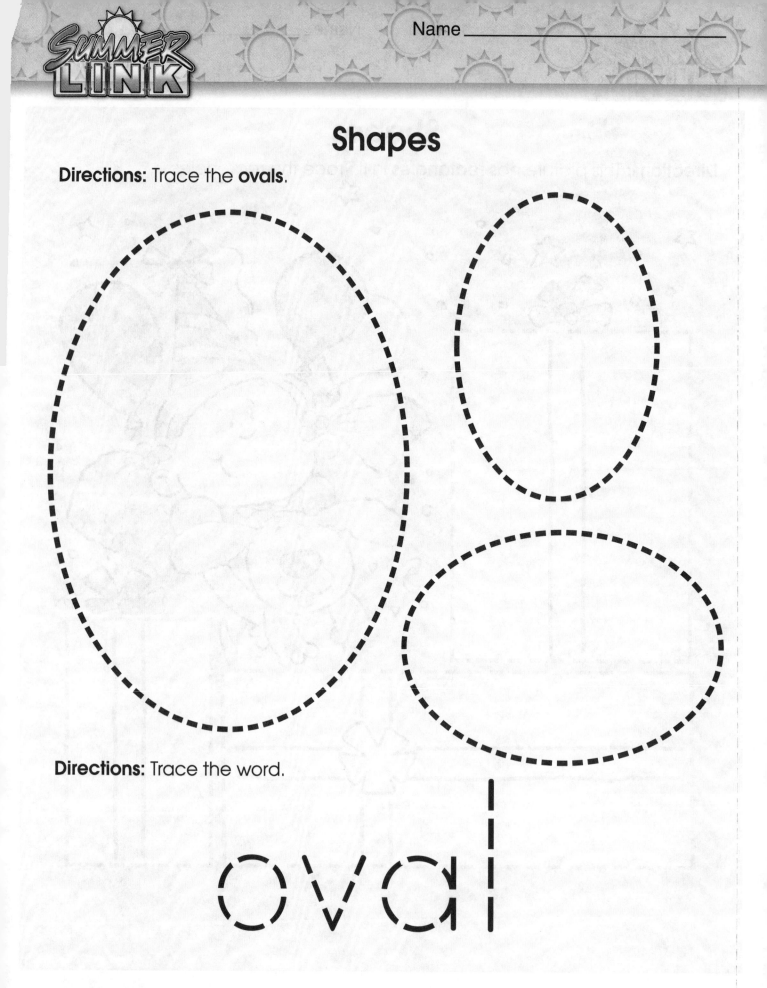

Directions: Trace the word.

oval

Shapes

Directions: This picture has **ovals** in it. Trace the ovals.

Shapes

Directions: Trace the **diamonds**.

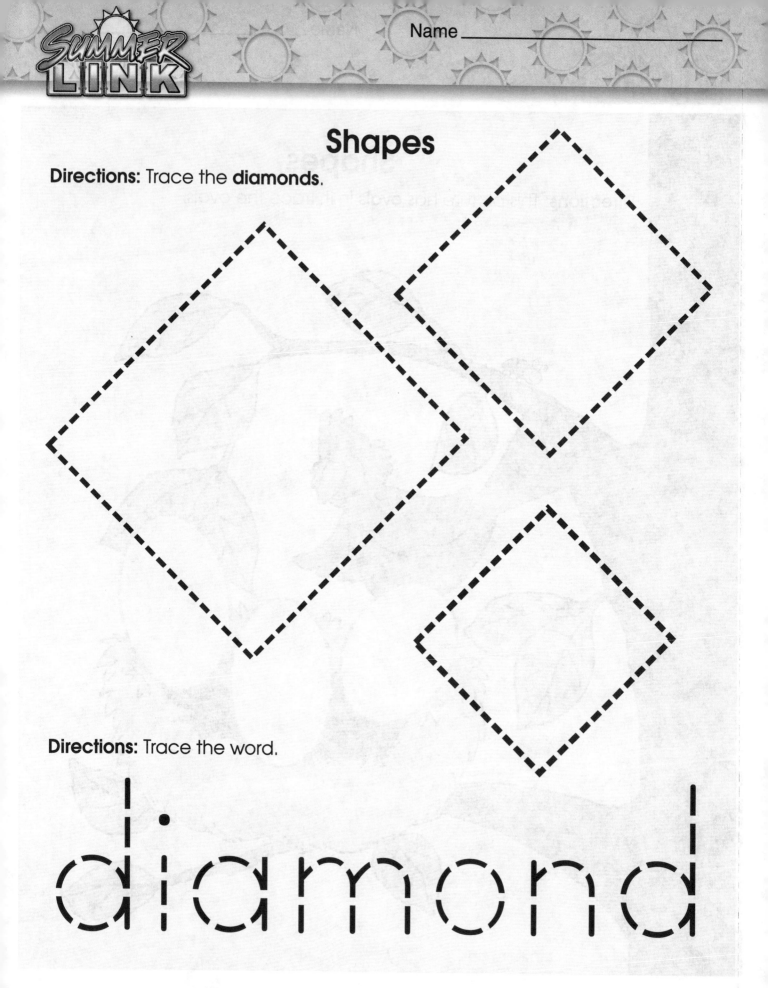

Directions: Trace the word.

diamond

Shapes

Directions: This picture has **diamonds** in it. Trace the diamonds.

Review Shapes

Directions: Draw a line to match each shape on the left to the same shape on the right.

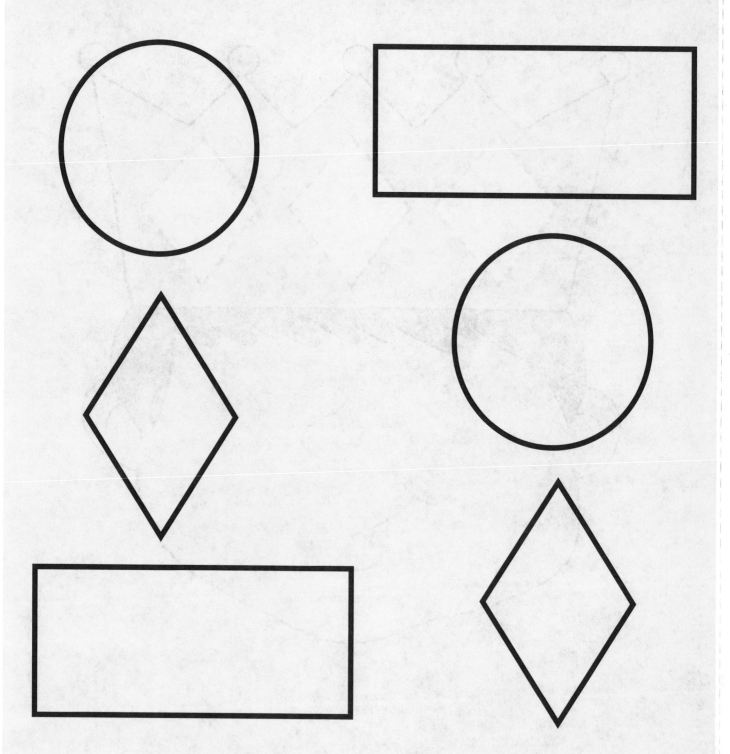

Review Shapes

Directions: Draw a line to match each shape on the left to a picture with the same shape on the right.

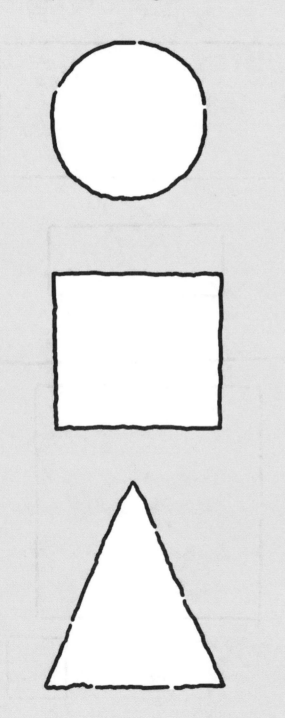

Big and Small

Directions: Color the **big** shape in each box. Draw a line under the **small** shape in each box.

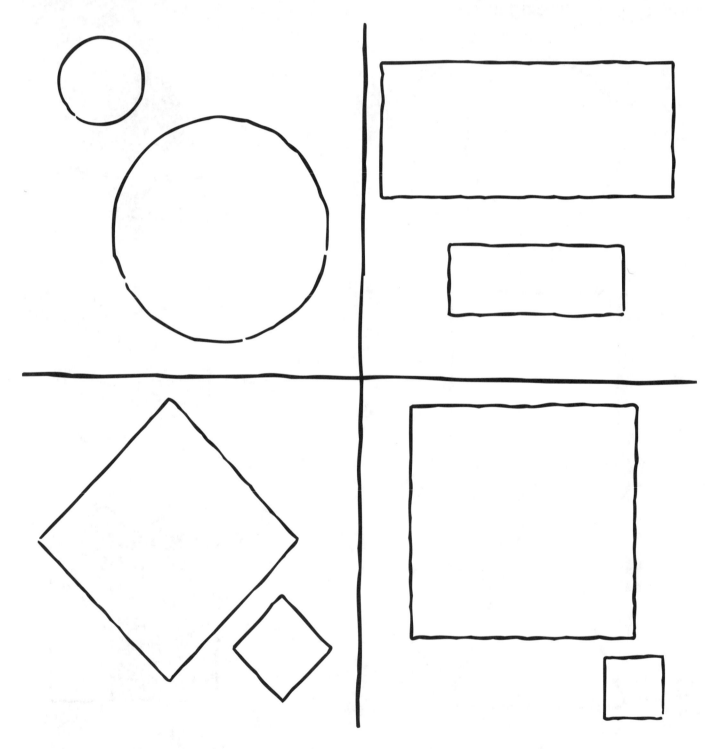

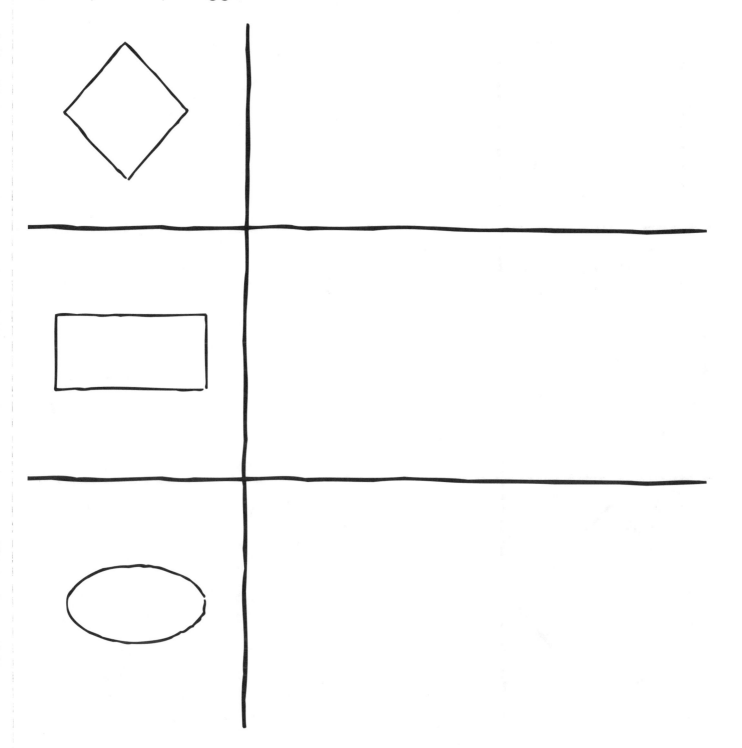

Bigger

Directions: Name the shape in each box. Then draw the same shape again. Make your shape **bigger** than the one in the box.

Smaller

Directions: Name the shape in each box. Then draw the same shape again. Make your shape **smaller** than the one in the box.

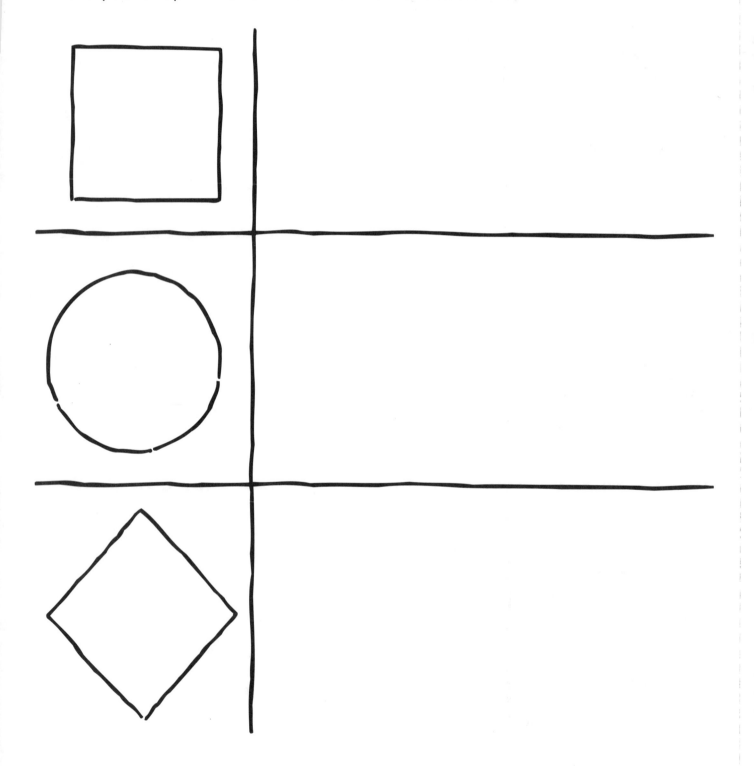

Shape Patterns

Directions: Circle the shape that comes next in each pattern.

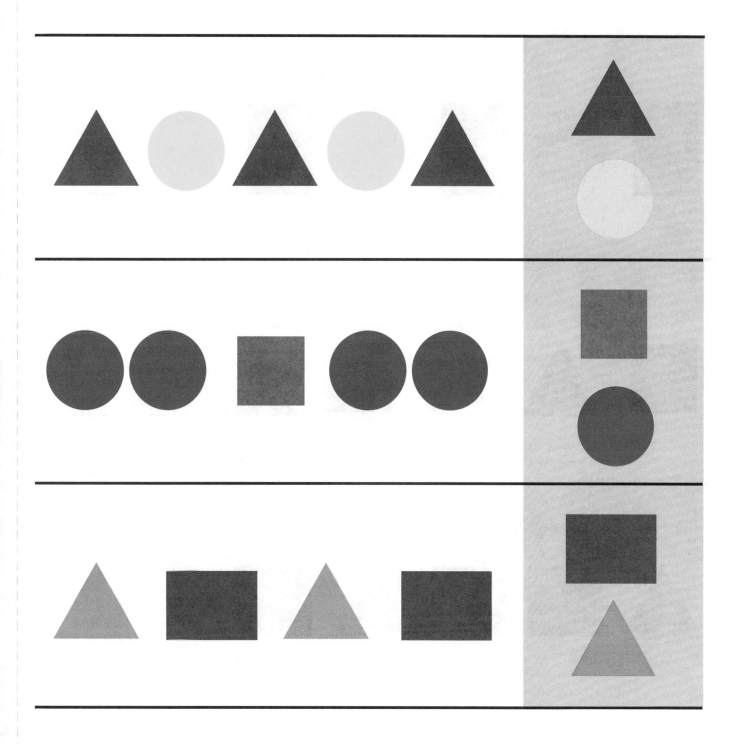

Shape Patterns

Directions: Draw and color the shape that comes next in each pattern.

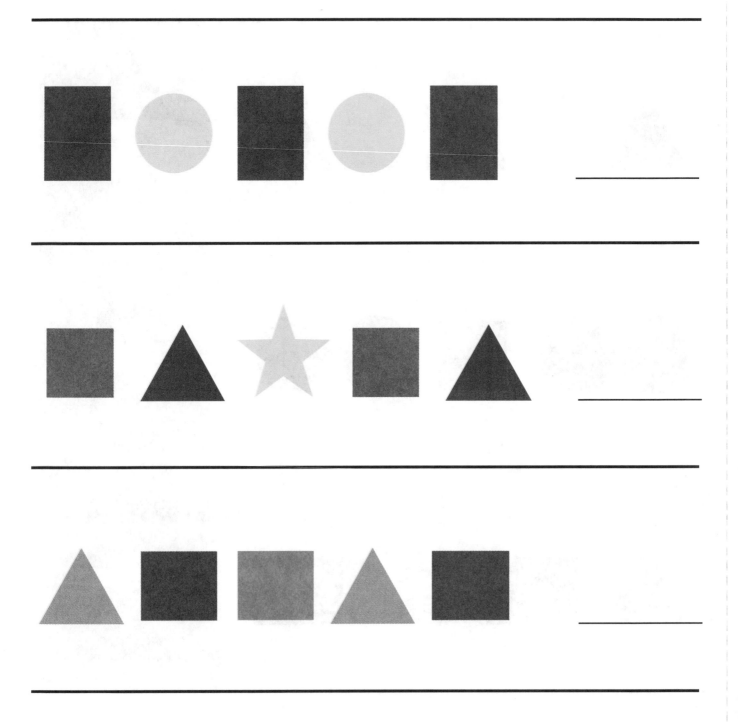

Counting

Directions: Look at the numbers. Count to 10.

Directions: Trace the number **0**.

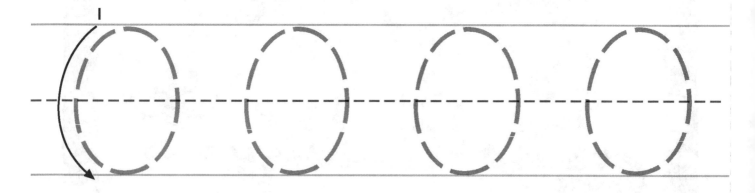

Now, write the number **0**.

zero

Directions: Trace the word **zero**.

zero zero

Now, write the word **zero**.

0 zero

Directions: Color the fish with **0** spots orange.

0 zero

Directions: Circle the fishbowls with **0** fish in them. Write **0** on the line beside them.

Directions: Trace the number **1**.

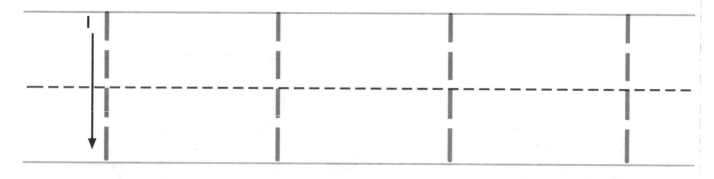

Now, write the number **1**.

Directions: Trace the word **one**.

Now, write the word **one**.

I • one

Directions: Circle **I** picture in each box. Then write the number **I** on the line in each box.

I • one

Directions: Draw a line to match each number **I** to one thing.

Directions: Trace the number **2**.

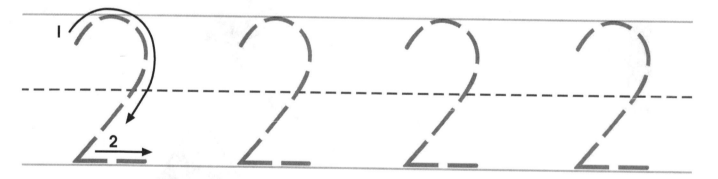

Now, write the number **2**.

Directions: Trace the word **two**.

t w o   t w o

Now, write the word **two**.

2 •• two

Directions: Color to find something that comes in **twos**.
- Color the spaces with **2 yellow**.
- Color the spaces with **I blue**.

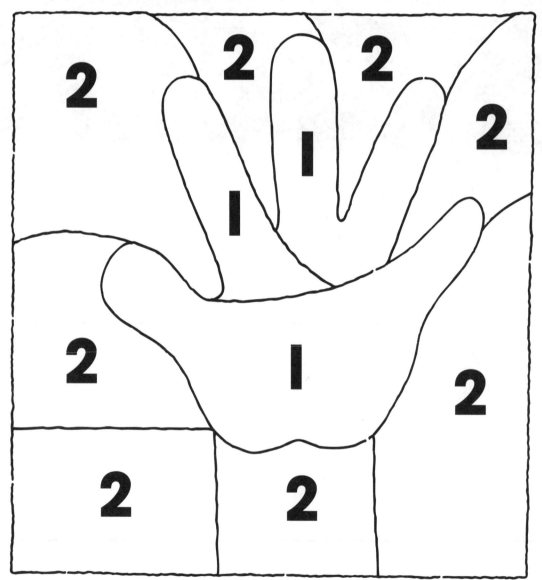

What did you find? _____

2 •• two

Directions: Circle **2** pictures in each box. Then write the number **2** on the line in each box.

45   Summer Link Super Edition Grade K

Directions: Trace the number **3**.

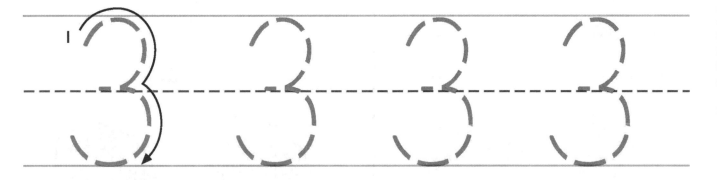

Now, write the number **3**.

Directions: Trace the word **three**.

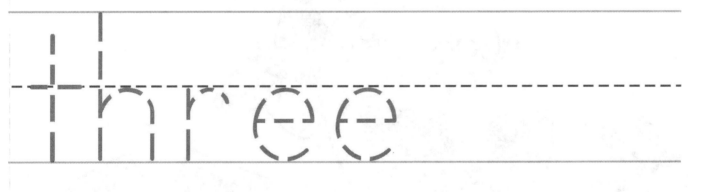

Now, write the word **three**.

3 ••• three

Directions: Circle **3** of each kind of cookie to go in the cookie jar.

3 ••• three

Directions: Count the number of pictures in each box. Circle the number that tells how many there are.

Summer Link Super Edition Grade K

Directions: Trace the number **4**.

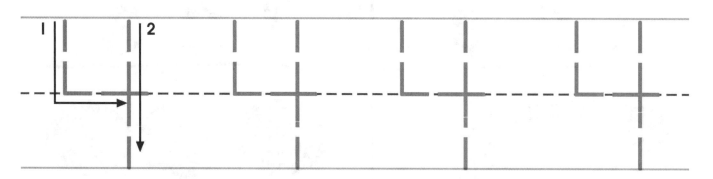

Now, write the number **4**.

Directions: Trace the word **four**.

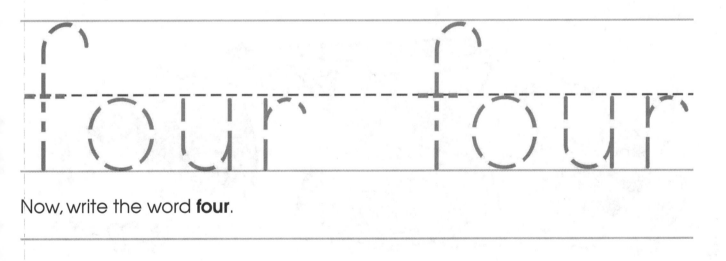

Now, write the word **four**.

4 •••• four

Directions: Draw **4** flowers in the vase.

Directions: Color to find the hidden picture.

- Color the spaces with **2 blue**.
- Color the spaces with **3 blue**.
- Color the spaces with **4 green**.

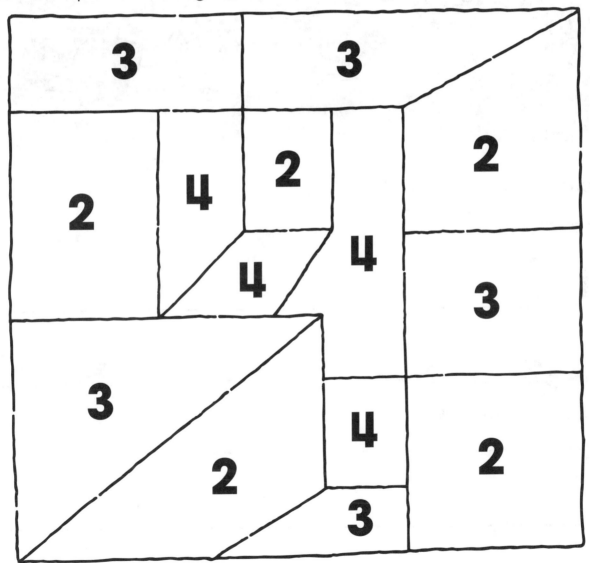

Directions: Trace the number **5**.

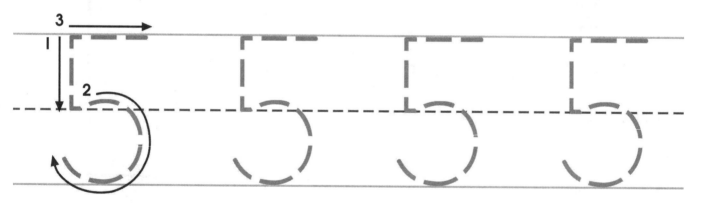

Now, write the number **5**.

five

Directions: Trace the word **five**.

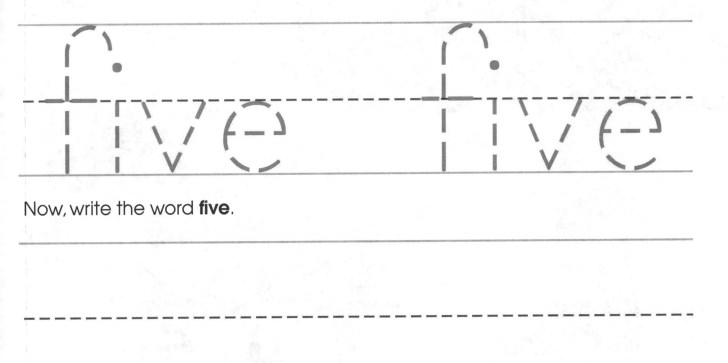

Now, write the word **five**.

5 ●●●●● five

Directions: Count how many there are in each group. Circle the number that tells how many there are.

5 ●●●●● five

Directions: Count the shapes. Then color and decorate the butterfly.

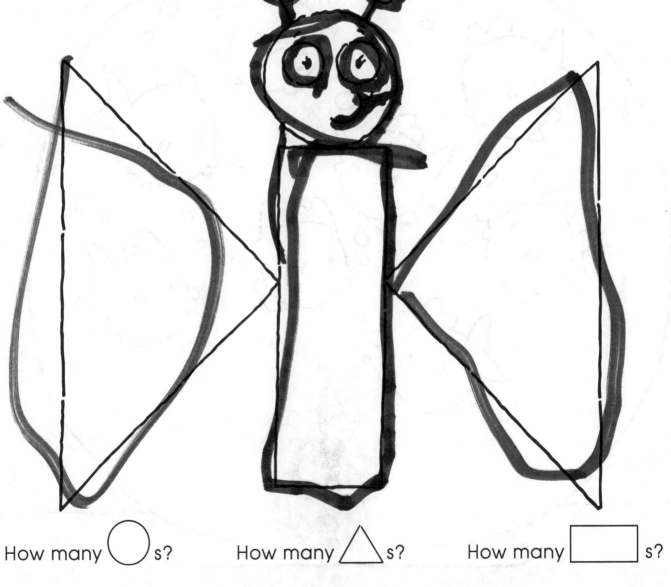

How many ◯s?   How many △s?   How many ▢s?

Name _____

Review Numbers 1-5

Directions: Follow the directions to color the picture below.

- Color **5** fish **orange**.
- Color **3** fish **brown**.
- Draw **2 pink** shells.
- Draw **1 yellow** starfish.

Review Numbers 1—5

Directions: Trace and write the missing numbers below.

Directions: Trace the number **6**.

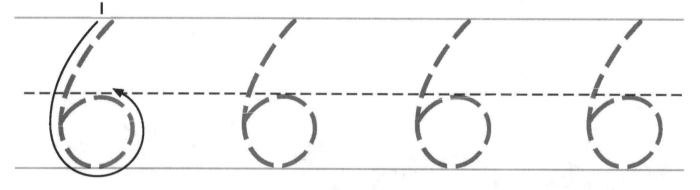

Now, write the number **6**.

Directions: Trace the word **six**.

Now, write the word **six**.

6 ⦁⦁⦁⦁⦁⦁ six

Directions: Count the number of dots on each gas pump.
Write the number on the line above each car.

_____

_____

_____

_____

6 ⬤⬤ six

Directions: Help the car get to the gas pump. Use a crayon to follow the path of **6**'s.

Directions: Trace the number **7**.

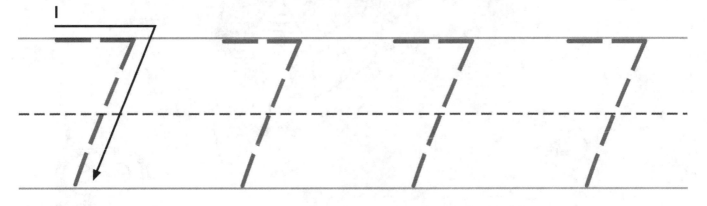

Now, write the number **7**.

Directions: Trace the word **seven**.

seven

Now, write the word **seven**.

7 ●●●●●●● seven

Directions: Circle **7** things on each shelf.

Directions: Color the picture to find a special treat.
- Color the spaces with **5 green.**
- Color the space with **6 brown.**
- Color the spaces with **7 pink.**

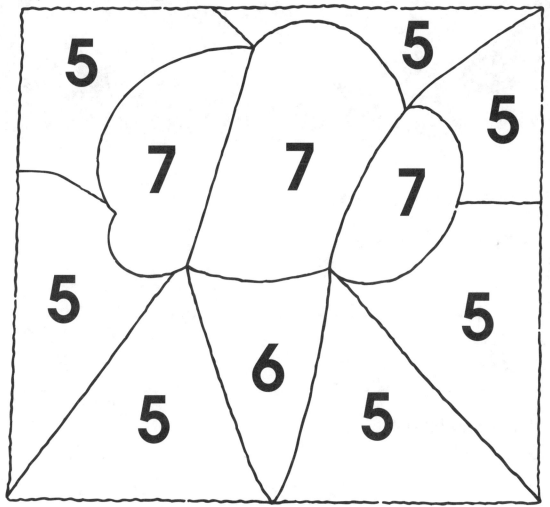

What did you find? _____

Directions: Trace the number **8**.

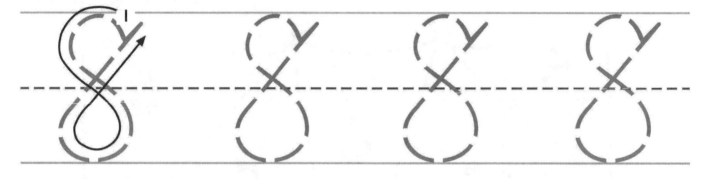

Now, write the number **8**.

Directions: Trace the word **eight**. Now, write the word **eight**.

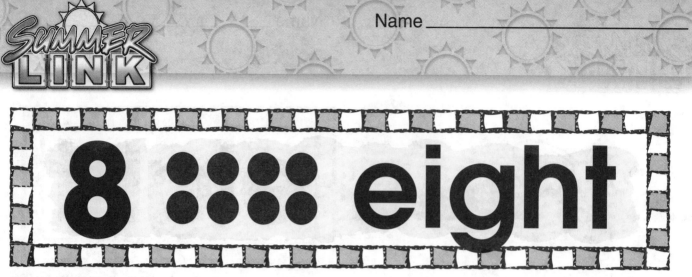

Directions: Put these **8** shoes into pairs. Draw a line to match each shoe on the left with a shoe that is the same on the right.

8 ●●●● eight

Directions: Count and circle **8** legs on each caterpillar.

Directions: Trace the number **9**.

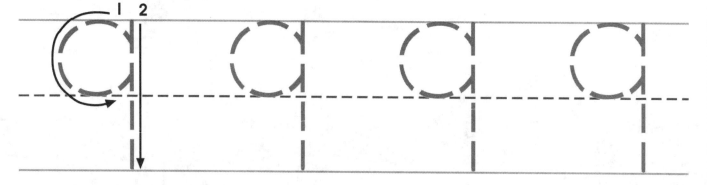

Now, write the number **9**.

Directions: Trace the word **nine**.

Now, write the word nine.

9 •••••• nine

Directions: Circle **9** bugs in each group.

74

9 ••••••••• nine

Directions: Draw **9** black dots on the ladybug's back.

Directions: Trace the number **10**.

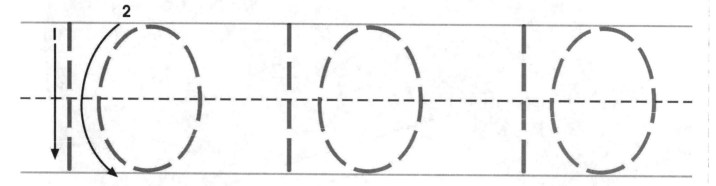

Now, write the number **10**.

Directions: Trace the word **ten**.

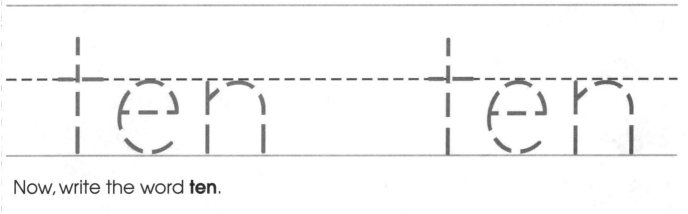

Now, write the word **ten**.

10 ●●●●● ten

Directions: Follow the directions to color the butterfly.
- Color **5** dots **red**.
- Color **3** dots **blue**.
- Color **2** dots **orange**.

Count the dots on the butterfly.
How many are there altogether? _____

Name _____

10 ●●●●● ten

Directions: Draw **10** legs on the caterpillar.

Review Numbers 1—10

Directions: Count your fingers on both hands. Write the numbers.

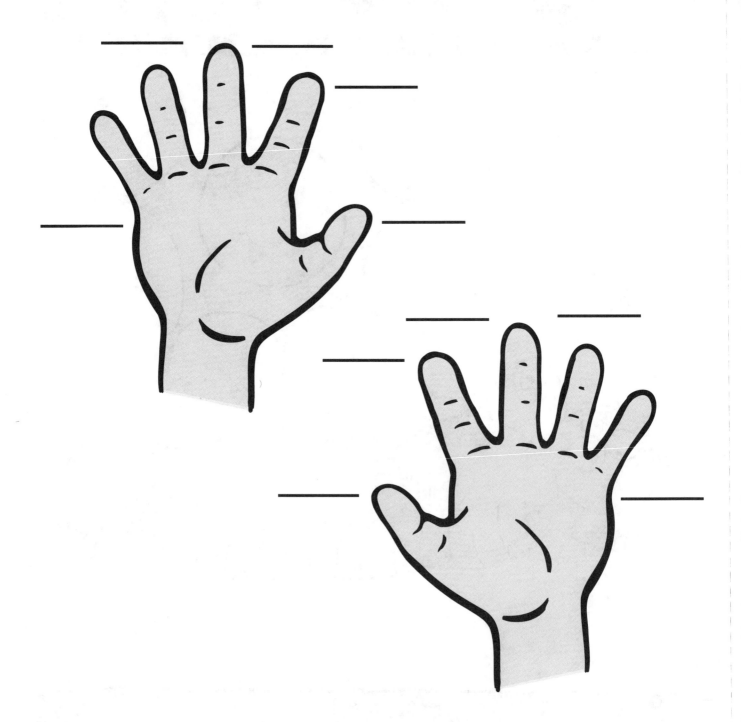

Review Numbers 1—10

Directions: Count your toes on both feet. Write the numbers.

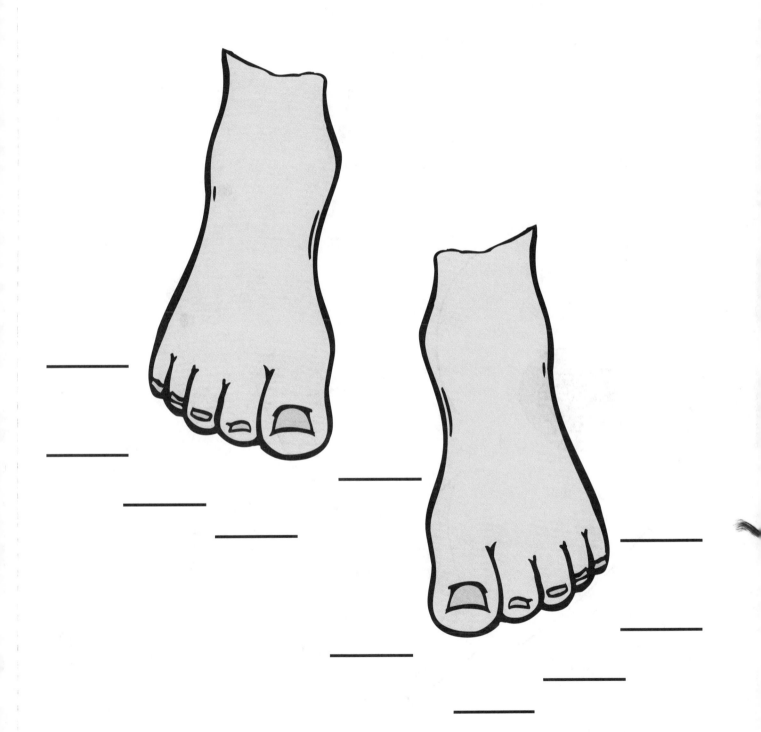

Review Numbers 1—10

Directions: Connect the dots from **1** to **10**. Then color the picture. What is it?

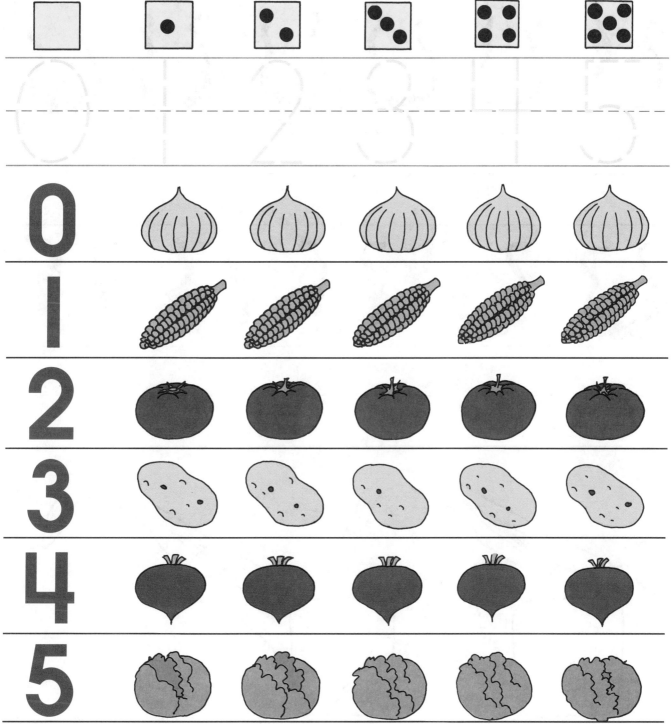

Order 0—5

Directions: Trace the numbers **0—5** in order. Circle the vegetables to show the numbers.

Summer Link Super Edition Grade K

Order 0—10

Directions: Count each group of beads and trace the numbers. Complete the dot-to-dot. Connect the dots in order from 0 to 10. Color the object. What is it?

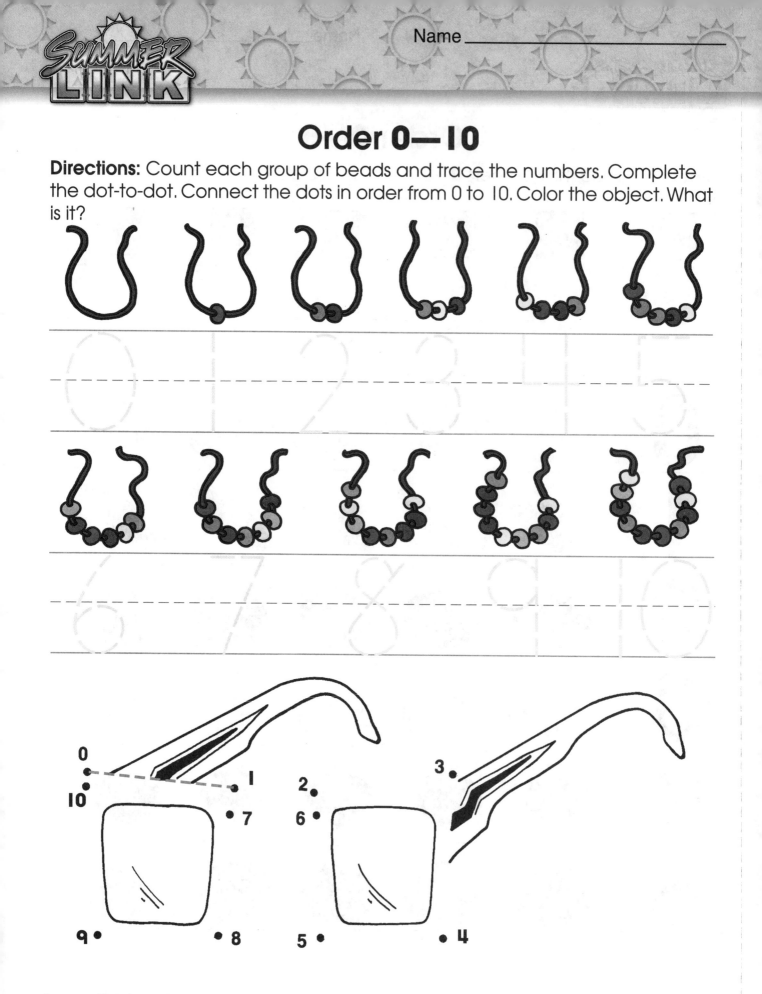

Name _____

Missing Numbers

Directions: Samantha is learning her numbers. In each set of boxes, there is a number missing. The missing number should be between the other two numbers. Write the missing numbers for Samantha below. Samantha has done the first one.

Summer Link Super Edition Grade K

More Missing Numbers

Directions: Write the missing number.

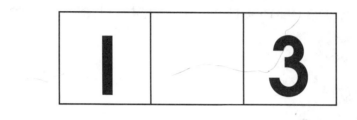

| 1 | | 3 |

| 8 | | 10 |

| 6 | | 8 |

Directions: Draw a circle around the number that is smaller in each pair.

| 10 | 4 | | 2 | 7 | | 5 | 1 |

One for Each

Directions: Each animal needs a home. Draw a line to match each animal with a home.

Same Number

Directions: Color the pictures that have the same number of things in each box.

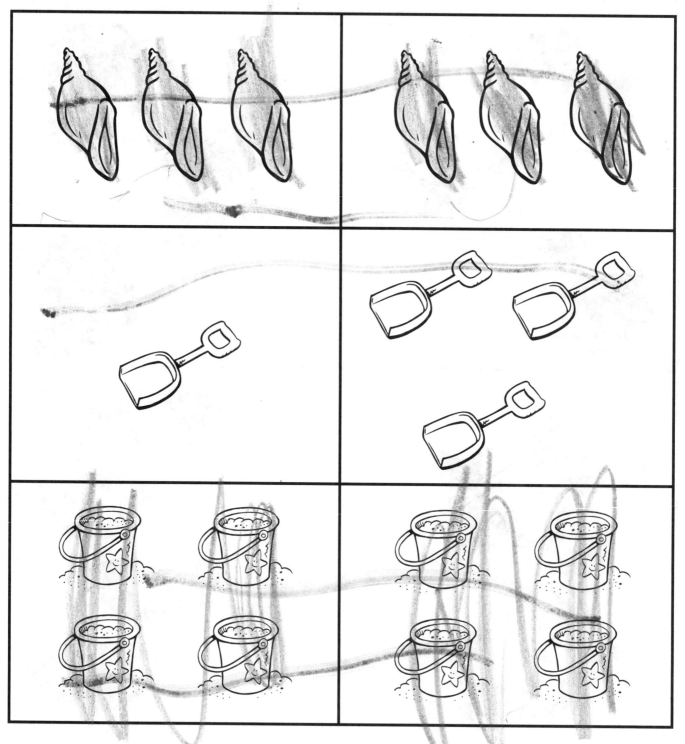

More and Fewer

Directions: Count the blocks in each group. Circle the group of blocks that has **more**.

Name _____

More and Fewer

Directions: Count the cars in each box. Circle the group in each box that has **fewer** cars.

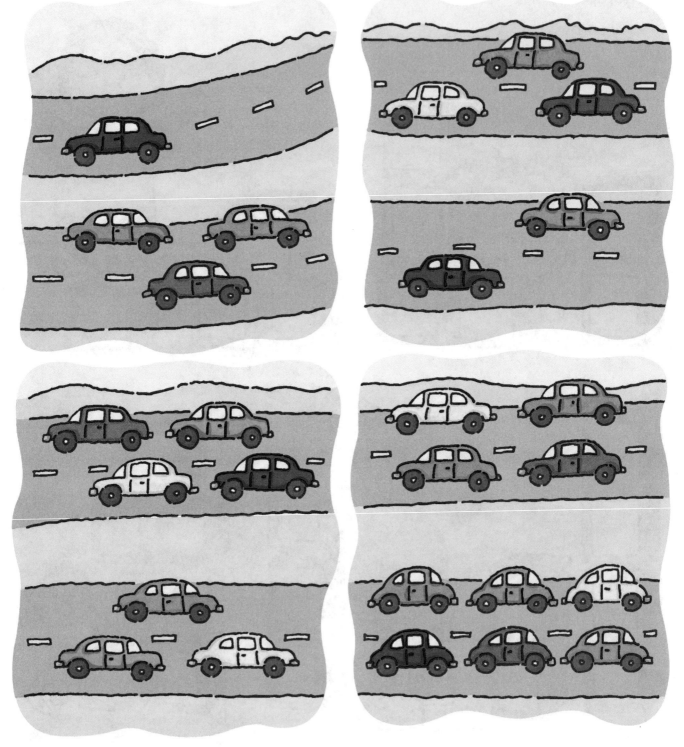

Name _____

More

Directions: Circle the group in each box that has **more.**

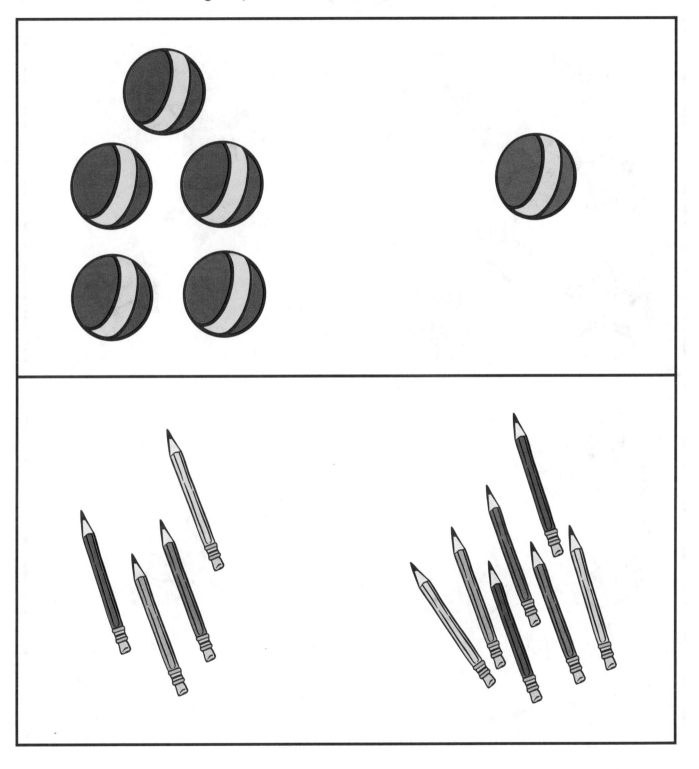

Summer Link Super Edition Grade K

Fewer

Directions: Circle the group in each box that has **fewer**.

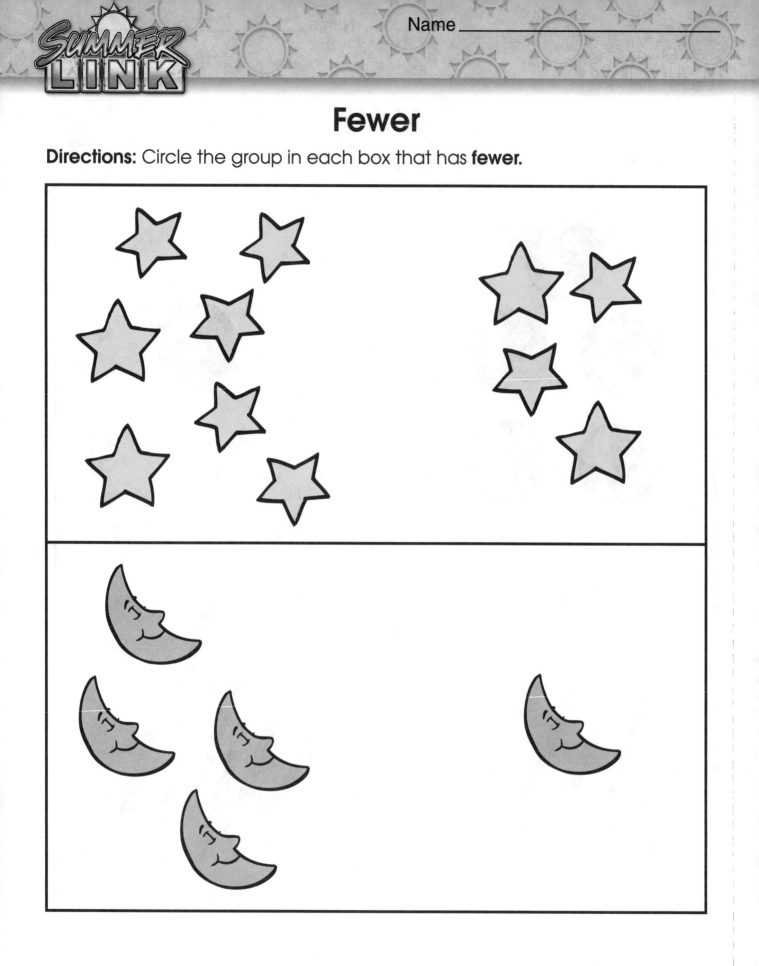

Art Class

Directions: It's time for Mrs. Murky's class to do art. Mrs. Murky has placed scissors, boxes of crayons, sheets of paper, and balls of clay on her desk.

• How many **scissors** are on Mrs. Murky's desk? _____

• How many **boxes of crayons** are on Mrs. Murky's desk? _____

• How many **sheets of paper** are on Mrs. Murky's desk? _____

• How many **balls of clay** are on Mrs. Murky's desk? _____

Number Quilt

Directions: All the monsters love to do math. Look at this quilt they made. The numbers **0** through **9** are hidden in the squares. Can you help the monsters find them? Color in each number.

Page 14

Page 15

Page 16

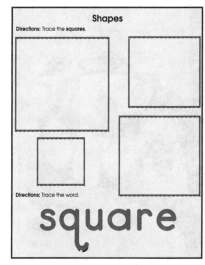

Page 17

Page 18

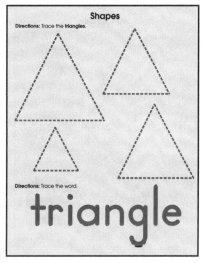

Page 19

Page 20

Page 21

Page 22

95   Summer Link Super Edition Grade K

Page 23

Page 24

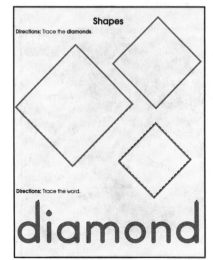

Page 25

Page 26

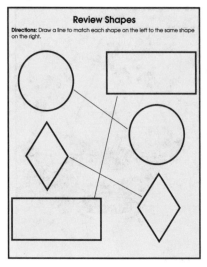

Page 27

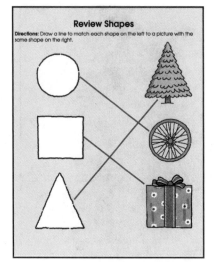

Page 28

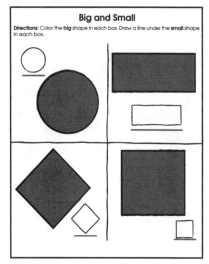

Page 29

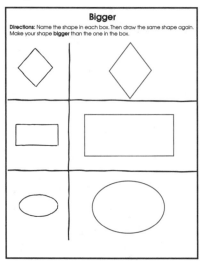

Page 30

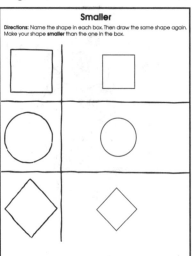

Page 31

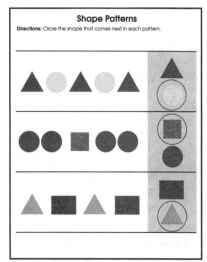

Page 22

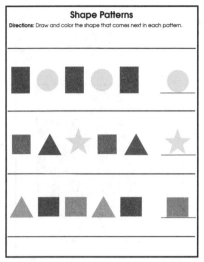

Shape Patterns

Directions: Draw and color the shape that comes next in each pattern.

Page 24

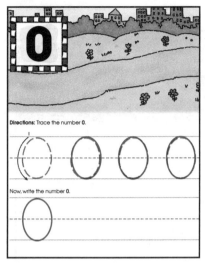

Directions: Trace the number **0**.

Now, write the number **0**.

Page 25

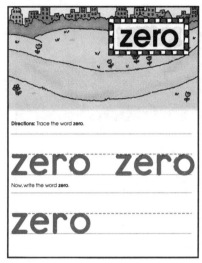

zero

Directions: Trace the word **zero**.

zero zero

Now, write the word **zero**.

zero

Page 26

0 zero

Directions: Color the fish with **0** spots orange.

Page 27

0 zero

Directions: Circle the fishbowls with **0** fish in them. Write **0** on the line beside them.

0

0

Page 28

1

Directions: Trace the number 1.

Now, write the number 1.

Page 29

one

Directions: Trace the word **one**.

one one

Now, write the word **one**.

one

Page 30

1 • one

Directions: Circle **1** picture in each box. Then write the number **1** on the line in each box.

Page 31

1 • one

Directions: Draw a line to match each number **1** to one thing.

Page 32

Directions: Trace the number **2**.

2 2 2 2 2

Now, write the number **2**.

2

Page 33

Directions: Trace the word **two**.

two two

Now, write the word **two**.

two

Page 34

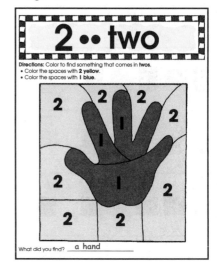

Directions: Color to find something that comes in **twos**.
• Color the spaces with **2 yellow**.
• Color the spaces with **1 blue**.

What did you find? _a hand_

Page 35

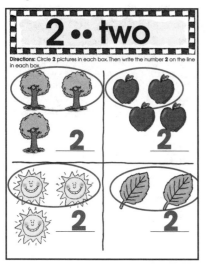

2 •• two

Directions: Circle **2** pictures in each box. Then write the number **2** on the line in each box.

Page 36

Directions: Trace the number **3**.

3 3 3 3

Now, write the number **3**.

3

Page 37

Directions: Trace the word **three**.

three

Now, write the word **three**.

three

Page 38

3 ••• three

Directions: Circle **3** of each kind of cookie to go in the cookie jar.

Page 39

3 ••• three

Directions: Count the number of pictures in each box. Circle the number that tells how many there are.

Page 40

Directions: Trace the number **4**.

Now, write the number **4**.

Page 41

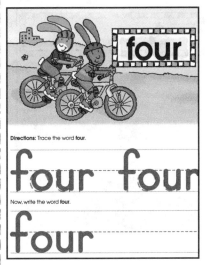

four

Directions: Trace the word **four**.

four four

Now, write the word **four**.

four

Page 42

4 •••• four

Directions: Draw 4 flowers in the vase.

Page 43

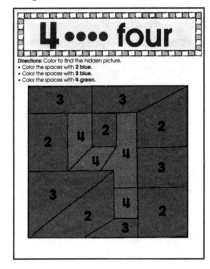

4 •••• four

Directions: Color to find the hidden picture.
• Color the spaces with **2 blue**.
• Color the spaces with **3 blue**.
• Color the spaces with **4 green**.

Page 44

5

Directions: Trace the number **5**.

5 5 5 5

Now, write the number **5**.

5

Page 45

five

Directions: Trace the word **five**.

five five

Now, write the word **five**.

five

Page 46

5 ••••• five

Directions: Count how many there are in each group. Circle the number that tells how many there are.

3 (4) 5   (3) 4 5

3 4 (5)

Page 47

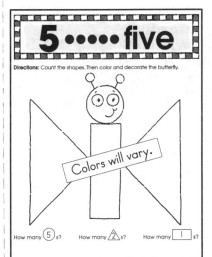

5 ••••• five

Directions: Count the shapes. Then color and decorate the butterfly.

Colors will vary.

How many (5) s?   How many /2\ s?   How many ☐ s?

Page 48

Review Numbers 1–5

Directions: Follow the directions to color the picture below.
• Color **5** fish **orange**.
• Color **3** fish **brown**.
• Draw **2 pink** shells.
• Draw **1 yellow** starfish.

Page 49

Review Numbers 1—5

Directions: Trace and write the missing numbers below.

1	2	3	4	5
1	2	3	4	5
1	2	3	4	5

Page 50

Page 51

Page 52

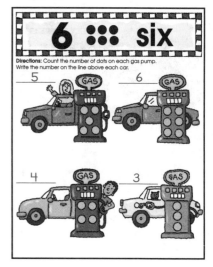

Page 53

Page 54

Page 55

Page 56

Page 57

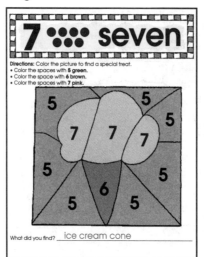

Page 58

Page 59

Page 60

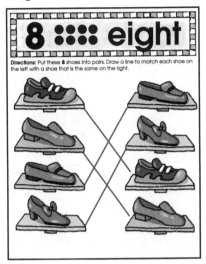

Page 61

Page 62

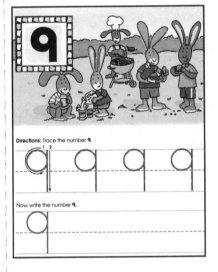

Page 63

Page 64

Page 65

Page 66

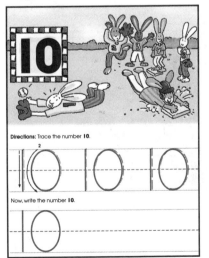

Page 67

Page 68

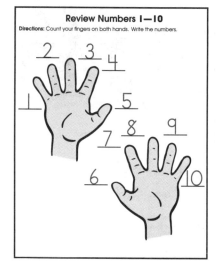

10 ::::: ten

Directions: Follow the directions to color the butterfly.
- Color **5** dots red.
- Color **3** dots blue.
- Color **2** dots orange.

Count the dots on the butterfly.
How many are there altogether? __10__

Page 69

10 ::::: ten

Directions: Draw **10** legs on the caterpillar.

Page 70

Review Numbers 1—10
Directions: Count your fingers on both hands. Write the numbers.

Page 71

Review Numbers 1—10
Directions: Count your toes on both feet. Write the numbers.

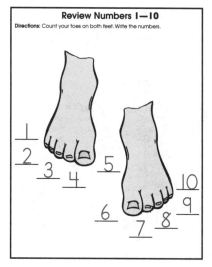

Page 72

Review Numbers 1—10
Directions: Connect the dots from 1 to 10. Then color the picture. What is it?

A fish

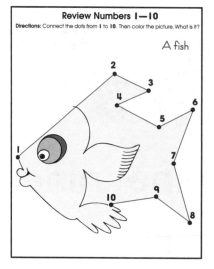

Page 73

Order 0—5
Directions: Trace the numbers **0—5** in order. Circle the vegetables to show the numbers.

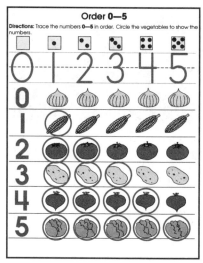

Page 74

Order 0—10
Directions: Count each group of beads and trace the numbers. Complete the dot-to-dot. Connect the dots in order from 0 to 10. Color the object. What is it?

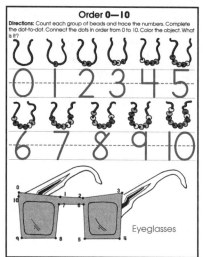

Eyeglasses

Page 75

Missing Numbers
Directions: Samantha is learning her numbers. In each set of boxes, there is a number missing. The missing number should be between the other two numbers. Write the missing numbers for Samantha below. Samantha has done the first one.

4 5 6

7 8 9

3 4 5

Page 76

More Missing Numbers
Directions: Write the missing number.

1 2 3

8 9 10

6 7 8

Directions: Draw a circle around the number that is smaller in each pair.

10 ④   ② 7   5 ①

Page 77

Page 78

Page 79

Page 80

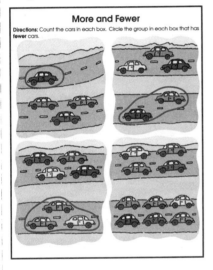

Page 81

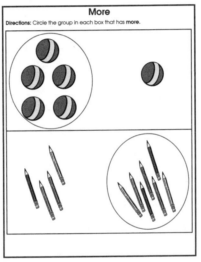

Page 82

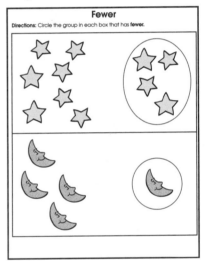

Page 83

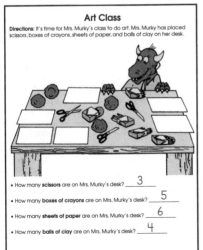

Page 84

Summer Link Super Edition Grade K

Numbers

Directions: Practice by tracing the words and numbers. Then write the words and numbers.

one 1

two 2

three 3

four 4

five 5

Numbers

Directions: Practice by tracing the words and numbers. Then write the words and numbers.

six 6

seven 7

eight 8

nine 9

ten 10

Numbers

Directions: Practice by tracing the words and numbers. Then write the words and numbers.

eleven 11

twelve 12

thirteen 13

fourteen 14

fifteen 15

Numbers

Directions: Practice by tracing the words and numbers. Then write the words and numbers.

sixteen 16

seventeen 17

eighteen 18

nineteen 19

twenty 20

Math Worksheet

Math Worksheet

Math Worksheet

Math Worksheet

Math Worksheet

Math Worksheet

This page intentionally left blank.

This page intentionally left blank.

Recommended Reading
Summer Before Kindergarten

- **Animal Babies 1 2 3**   Eve Spencer
- **Are You My Mother?**   P. D. Eastman
- **Chickens Aren't the Only Ones**   Ruth Heller
- **Count and See**   Tana Hoban
- **Duck in the Truck**   Jez Alborough
- **A Fishy Color Story**   Joanne and David Wylie
- **How Many Bugs in a Box?**   David Carter
- **If You Give a Moose a Muffin**   Laura J. Vumeroff
- **Just Like Daddy**   Frank Asch
- **My Daddy**   Mathew Price
- **My Many Colored Days**   Dr. Suess
- **My Mommy**   Mathew Price
- **The Napping House**   Audrey Wood
- **Numbers**   Monique Felix
- **Rainbow Fish**   Marcus Pfister
- **"Slowly, Slowly, Slowly," Said the Sloth**   Eric Carle
- **Ten Bears in Bed**   John Richardson
- **White Rabbit's Color Book**   Alan Baker

This page intentionally left blank.

Colors

Directions: Draw something that is **red**.

Now, trace the word **red**.

red

Colors

Directions: Circle the **yellow** picture in each row.

Colors

Directions: Draw something that is **blue**.

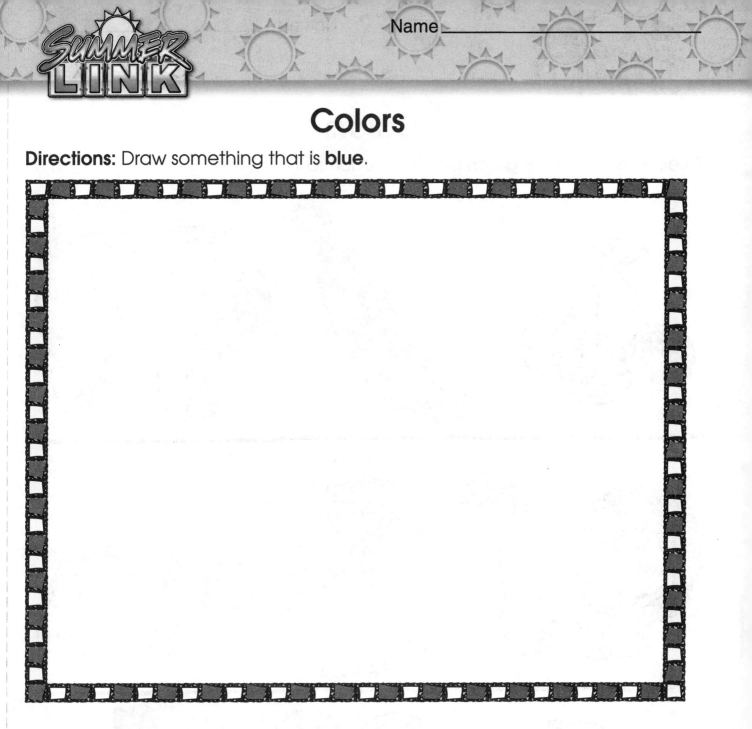

Now, trace the word **blue**.

blue

Summer Link Super Edition Grade K

Colors

Directions: Circle the **green** picture in each row.

Colors

Directions: Draw something that is **orange**.

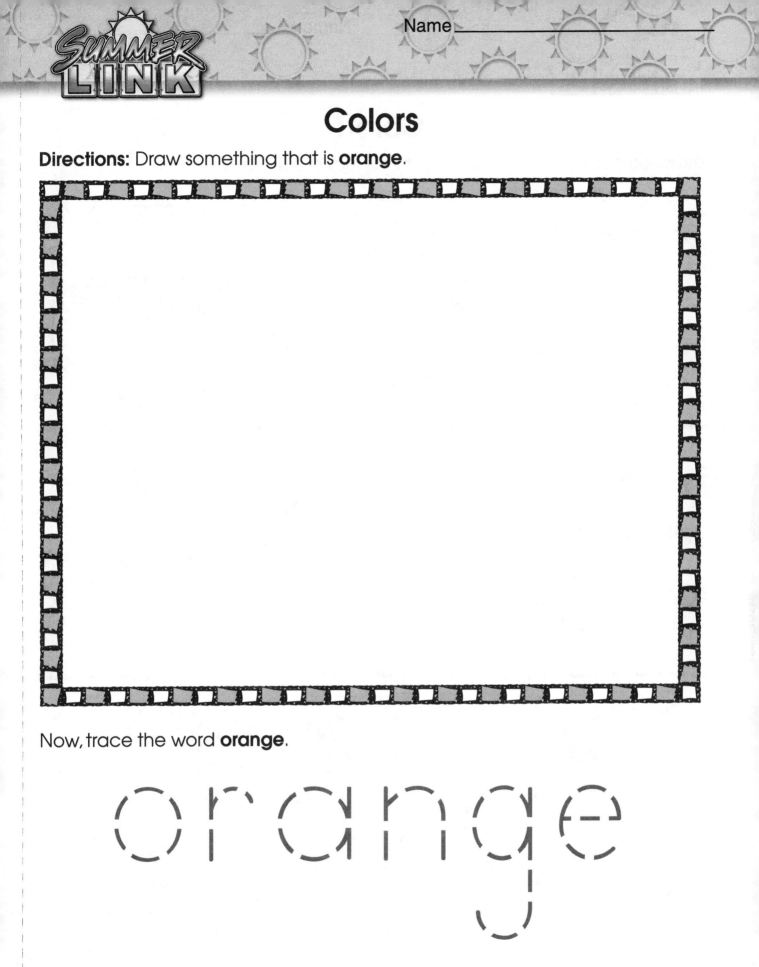

Now, trace the word **orange**.

Colors

Directions: In each row, color two things that are the same color.

Colors

Directions: Draw a line to match each picture to the crayon with the same color.

Shapes

Directions: This picture has **circles** in it. Trace the circles

Shapes

Directions: This picture has **squares** in it. Trace the squares.

Shapes

Directions: This picture has **triangles** in it. Trace the triangles.

Shapes

Directions: This picture has **rectangles** in it. Trace the rectangles.

Shapes

Directions: This picture has **ovals** in it. Trace the ovals.

Shapes

Directions: This picture has a **diamond** in it. Trace the diamond.

131   Summer Link Super Edition Grade K

Same Size

Directions: Circle the shape in each row that is the **same size** as the first shape.

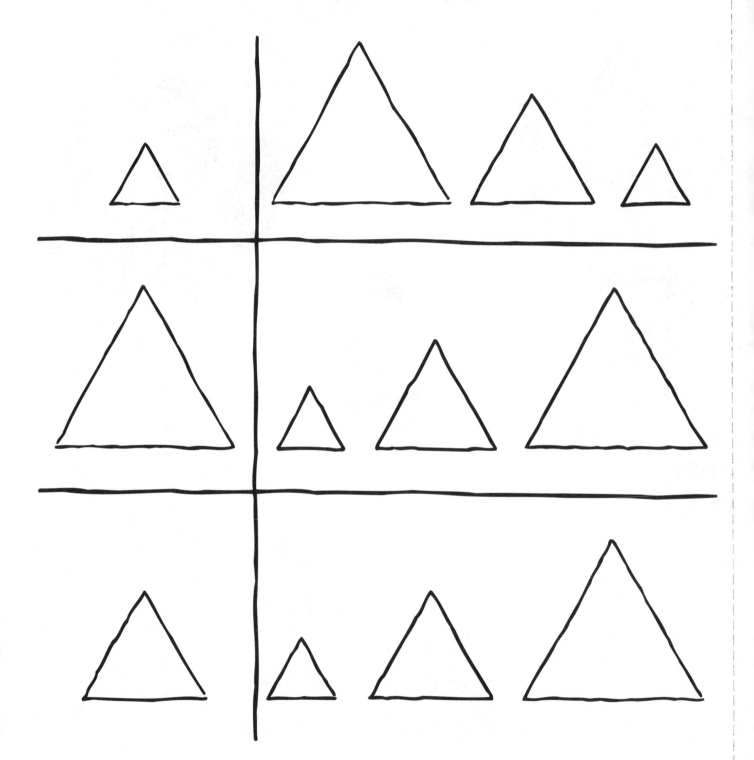

Name _____

Big and Small

Directions: Draw a line to match the shapes that are the same. Then color each **big** shape red and each **small** shape green.

Name _____

Shorter

Directions: Look at the glass below. Draw another glass beside it. Make your glass **shorter** than the first one.

Name _____

Taller

Directions: Look at the house on the left. Draw a roof on the house beside it. Make the roof on the other house **taller** than the first one.

Short and Tall

Directions: Circle each **short** person below. Draw a line under each **tall** person.

Name _____

Long and Short

Directions: Circle each **long** thing. Then draw a line under each **short** thing.

Review Size

Directions: Color the **longest** crayon **red**. Color the **shortest** crayon **purple**.

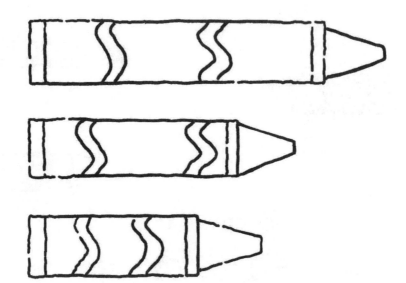

Directions: Circle two bears that are the **same size**.

Same

Directions: Look at the pictures in each row. Circle the picture that is the **same** as the first picture in each row.

Same

Directions: Look at the pictures in each row. Circle the picture that is the **same** as the first picture in each row.

Different

Directions: Look at the pictures in each row. Circle the picture that is **different** in each row.

Different

Directions: Look at the pictures in each row. Circle the picture that is **different** in each row.

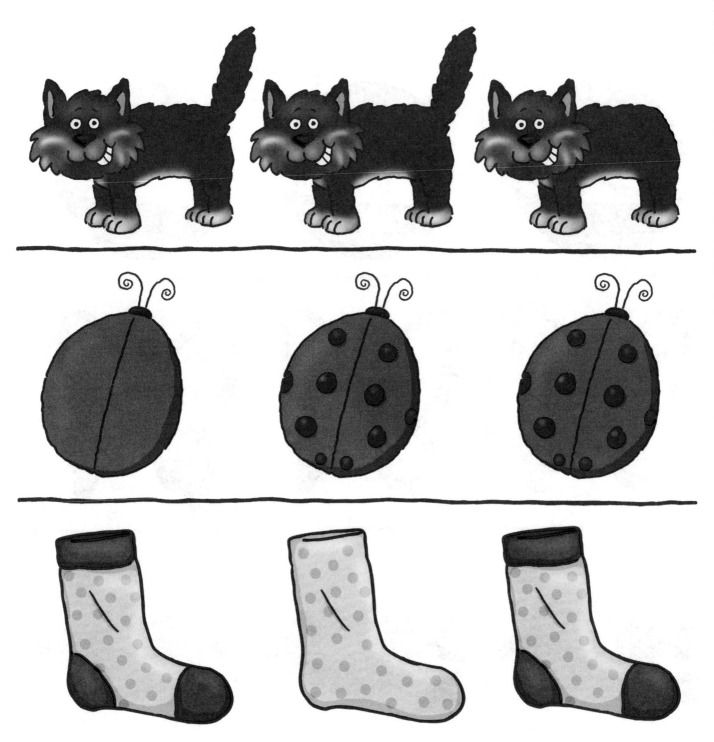

Opposites

Directions: Draw a picture of the opposite.

day	night
sad	happy

Left and Right

Directions: Color the pictures on the left green. Color the pictures on the right orange.

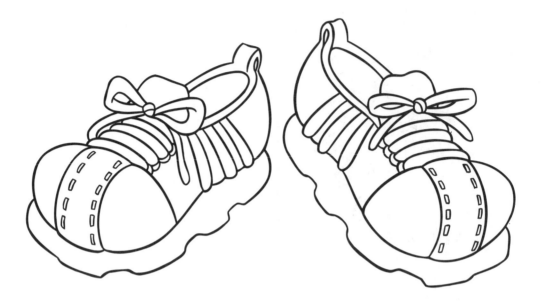

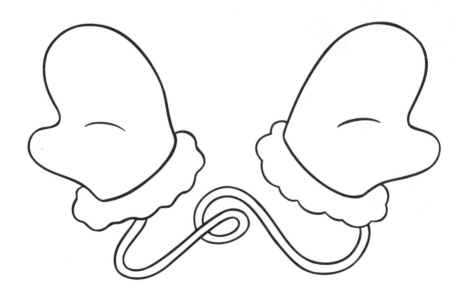

Animal Matching

Directions: Play a matching game with animals.

1. Cut out the pictures below and on the next page. Put them in a paper bag. Then shake the bag.
2. Pull out 2 pictures. If they are the same, keep them.
3. If the pictures are different, put them back in the bag and try again.
4. When you have matched all the cards, the game is over.

This page was left intentionally
blank for cutting activity on
previous page.

Summer Link Super Edition Grade K

This page was left intentionally
blank for cutting activity on
previous page.

Aa, Bb, Cc

Directions: Circle the letters in each row that match the first letter.

A	N	A	V	A
a	b	a	c	a
B	B	C	B	A
b	d	a	b	a
C	O	C	D	C
c	a	c	c	o

Dd, Ee, Ff

Directions: Look at the uppercase letter in each row. Color each picture with a matching lowercase letter.

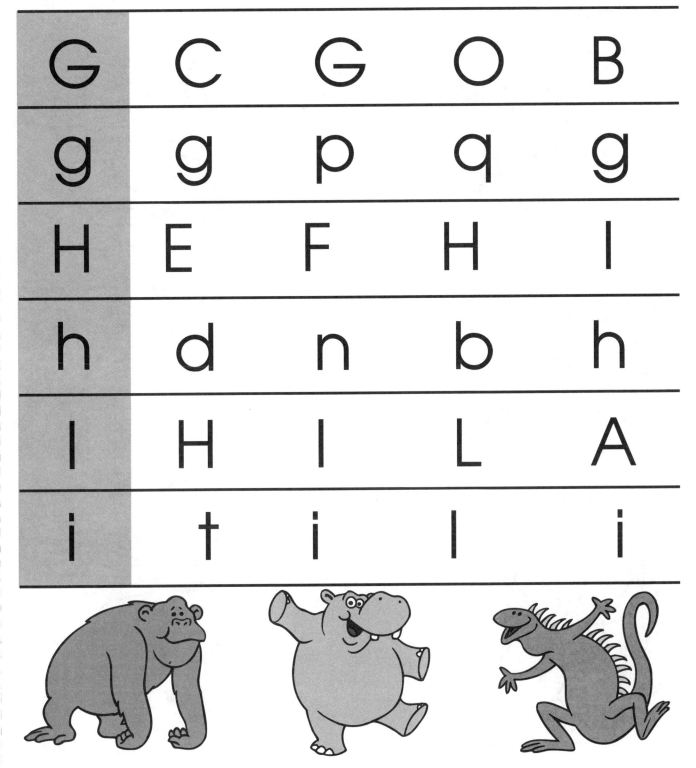

Name _____

Gg, Hh, Ii

Directions: Circle the letters in each row that match the first letter.

G	C	G	O	B
g	g	p	q	g
H	E	F	H	I
h	d	n	b	h
I	H	I	L	A
i	t	i	l	i

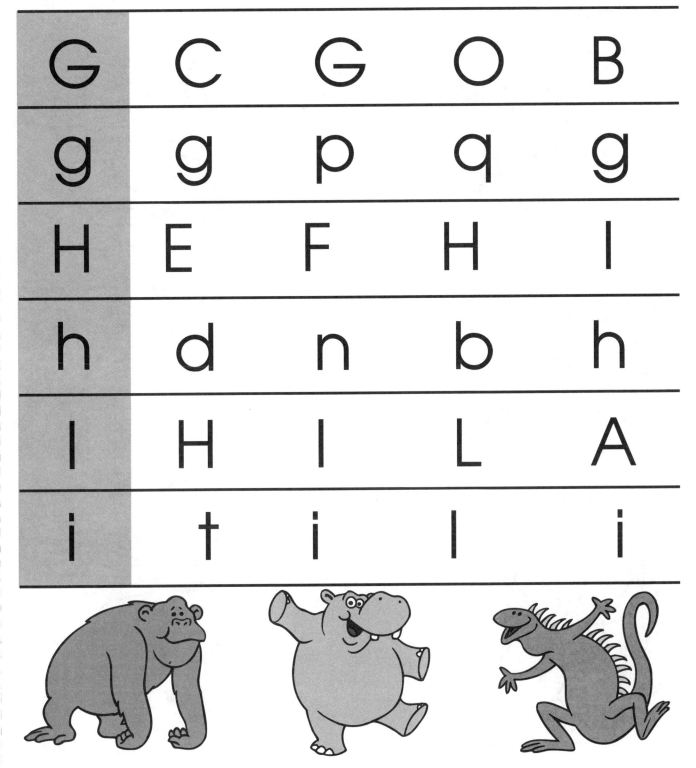

                    Summer Link Super Edition Grade K

Jj, Kk, Ll

Directions: Draw a line from each uppercase letter to its matching lowercase letter. Then color the pictures.

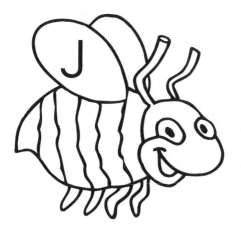

Review Aa–Mm

Directions: Help Adam get to the playground. Follow the letters in ABC order.

Mm, Nn, Oo

Directions: Circle the letters in each row that match the first letter.

M	H	M	n	L
m	M	a	m	n
N	M	N	m	N
n	n	m	a	n
O	O	D	B	O
o	a	O	c	o

Pp, Qq, Rr

Directions: Circle the letters in each row that match the first letter.

P	D	P	O	b
p	p	d	q	b
Q	O	Q	G	Q
q	p	q	d	b
R	R	B	P	R
r	r	n	m	r

Review: Pp-Tt

Directions: Draw a line from each uppercase letter to its matching lowercase letter.

Ss, Tt, Uu

Directions: Circle the letters in each row that match the first letter.

S	P	S	B	S
s	o	a	s	e
T	I	P	L	T
t	f	l	t	i
U	U	D	U	O
u	u	n	m	n

Vv, Ww, Xx

Directions: Circle the letters in each row that match the first letter.

V	W	V	A	N
V	w	x	v	y
W	V	M	A	W
w	w	v	x	m
X	Y	X	V	K
x	y	k	x	z

Yy, Zz

Directions: Circle the letters in each row that match the first letter.

Y	W	Y	V	X
y	w	x	v	y
Z	N	M	Z	W
z	n	z	x	m

ABC Order

Directions: Connect the dots in ABC order. Color the picture.

Left to Right

Directions: Help the bear get to the honey. Follow the arrow to trace a path to the honey.

Directions: Help the cow get to the grass. Follow the arrow to trace a path to the grass.

Top to Bottom

Directions: Help the firefighters get to the fire. Trace the lines from top to bottom.

Curved Lines

Directions: Trace each ocean wave from left to right. Then draw an ocean wave of your own.

Name _____

Top-to-Bottom Lines

Directions: Start at the top. Follow the arrows to trace the dotted lines.

Name _____

Slanted Lines

Directions: Start at the top. Follow the arrows to trace the dotted lines.

Curved Lines

Directions: Start at the dots on the left. Follow the arrows to trace the dotted lines.

Circles

Directions: Start at the dots on the left. Follow the arrows to trace the dotted lines.

Capital Letters

Directions: Names are special. We use **capital letters** to set them apart from other words. Circle the capital letters in the names below.

Jacob   Mary

Erik   Emily

Lisa   Tom

Ann   Fred

Now, write your name. Circle the capital letter.

_____

- - - - - - - - - - - - - - - - - -

_____

Name _____

Capital Letters

Directions: Write your name. Draw a picture of yourself doing something you like.

_____

- -

_____

Summer Link Super Edition Grade K

Writing Your Address

Directions: Write your address. Draw a picture to show where you live.

Short Vowel Aa

Directions: Short Aa is the sound at the beginning of the word **alligator**. Color the pictures that begin with the **short Aa** sound.

Summer Link Super Edition Grade K

Beginning Consonant Bb

Directions: These pictures begin with the letter **Bb**. Color these pictures.

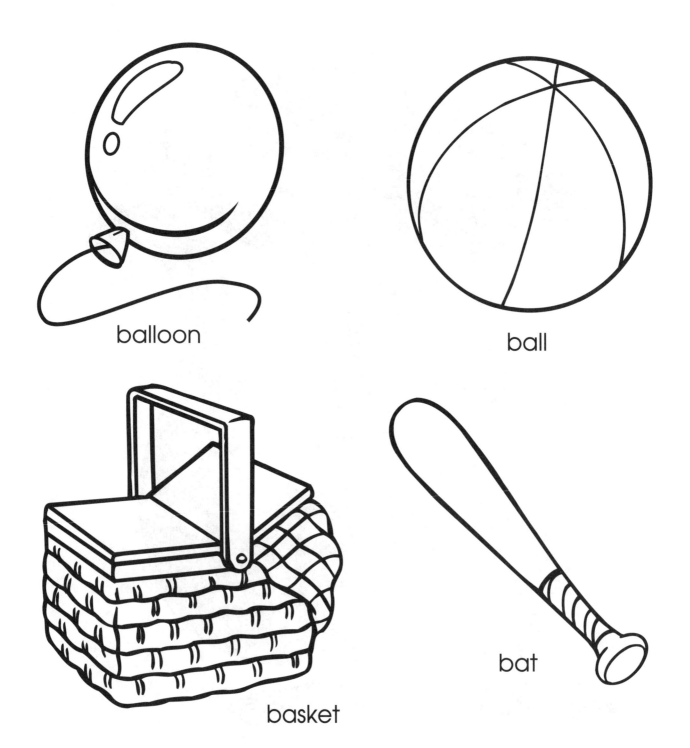

balloon

ball

basket

bat

Name _____

Beginning Consonant Cc

Directions: These pictures begin with the letter **Cc**. Color these pictures.

cat

coat

cookie

car

Beginning Consonant Dd

Directions: Say the picture names in each box on the door. Circle the picture whose name begins with the same sound as **dinosaur**.

Name _____

Short Vowel Ee

Directions: Short Ee is the sound in the middle of the word **hen**. Help the hen get to the barn. Follow the path with the pictures whose names have the **short Ee** sound.

Beginning Consonant Ff

Directions: Look at the bubbles below. Say each picture name. If the picture begins with the same sound as **fish**, color it blue.

Beginning Consonant Gg

Directions: Say each picture name. Circle the pictures whose names begin with the same sound as **goggles**.

Beginning Consonant Hh

Directions: Say each picture name. If the picture begins with the **Hh** sound, color the **hat**.

Short Vowel Ii

Directions: Read the words. Draw a line from each word to the picture that matches it.

Beginning Sounds Gg, Hh, Ii

Directions: Say the sound the letters make. Circle the pictures in each row that begin with the letter shown.

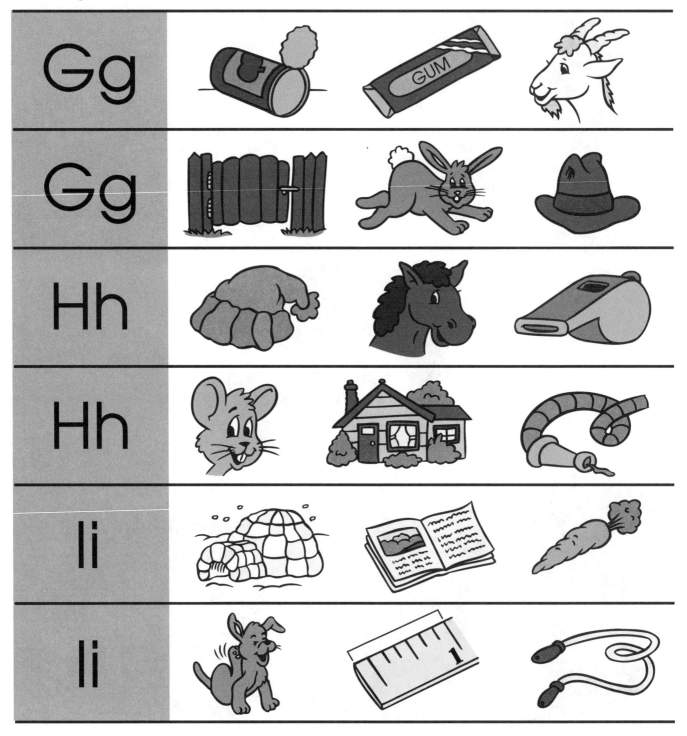

Beginning Consonant Jj

Directions: What is Jamie wearing today? Say each picture name. Color the spaces with the **Jj** sound blue. Color the other spaces yellow.

What is Jamie wearing? _____

Beginning Consonant Kk

Directions: Look at the pictures on the kite's tail. Say each picture name. If the picture begins with the same sound as **kite**, color it orange. Then color the kite.

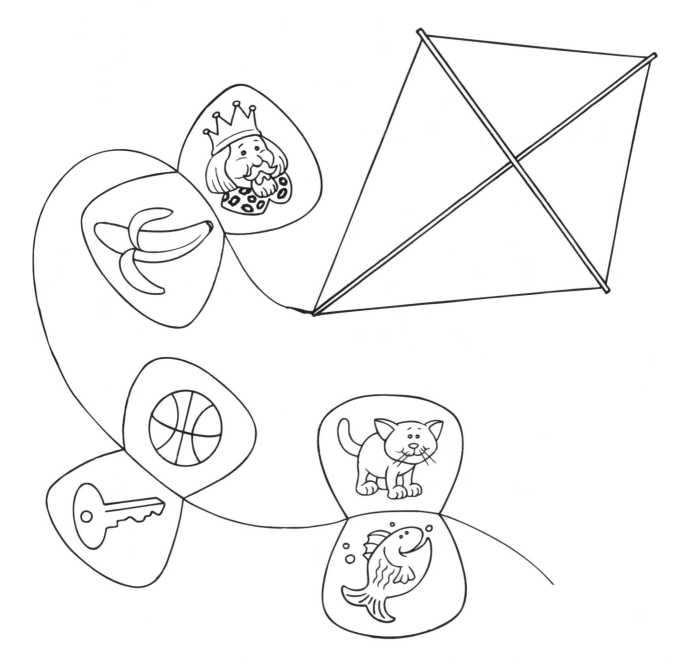

Beginning Consonant Ll

Directions: Cut out the stamps at the bottom of the page. Say each picture name. If the picture begins with the same sound as letter, glue it on an envelope.

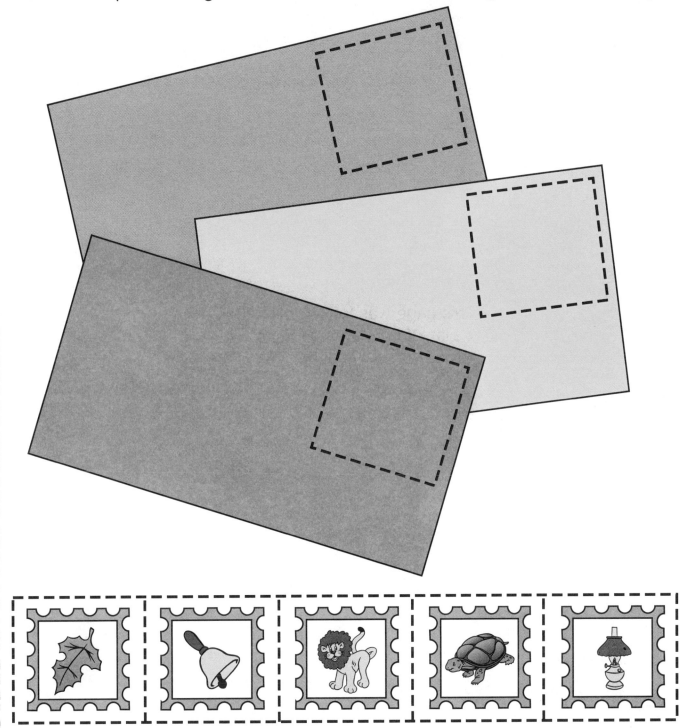

This page was left intentionally
blank for cutting activity on
previous page.

Beginning Consonant Mm

Directions: Say each picture name. Color the pictures whose names begin with the same sound as **macaroni** and **meatballs**.

Beginning Consonant Nn

Directions: Help the birds find their nest. Follow the path with the pictures whose names begin with the same sound as **nest**.

Short Vowel Oo

Directions: Write the letter **o** to complete each word. Read the words. Then find the pictures of the words at the bottom of the page and circle them.

f __ x   l __ g

d __ g   fr __ g

Beginning Consonant Pp

Directions: Pam only packs things whose names begin with the same sound as **panda**. Say the picture names. Circle each picture whose name begins with the same sound as **Pam** and **panda**.

Beginning Consonant Qq

Directions: Look at the pictures on the quilt below. Say each picture name. If the picture begins with the same sound as **quilt**, color the square yellow. Color the other squares purple.

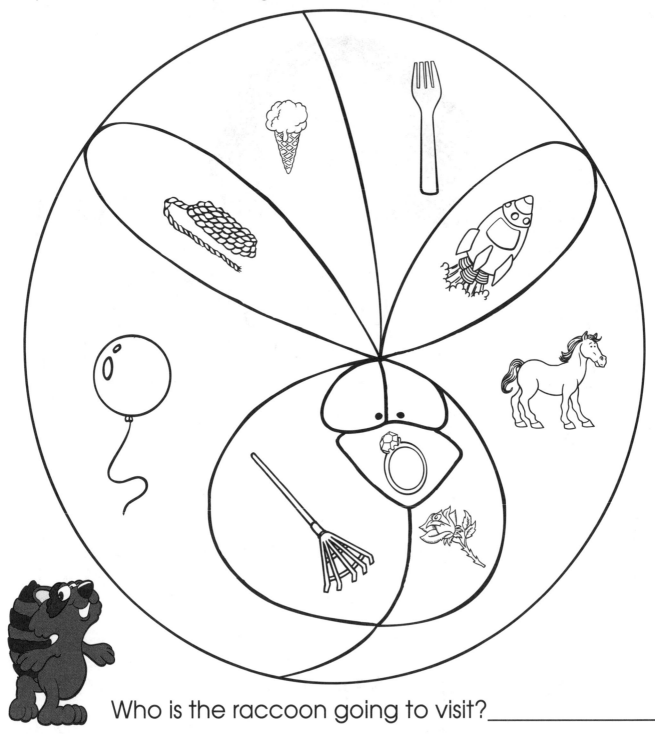

Beginning Consonant Rr

Directions: Who is the raccoon going to visit? Say each picture name. Color the pictures whose names begin with the same sound as **raccoon**.

Who is the raccoon going to visit?_____

Beginning Consonant Ss

Directions: Find the letter **S**. Say each picture name. If the picture begins with the same sound as **six**, color the space blue. Color the other spaces orange.

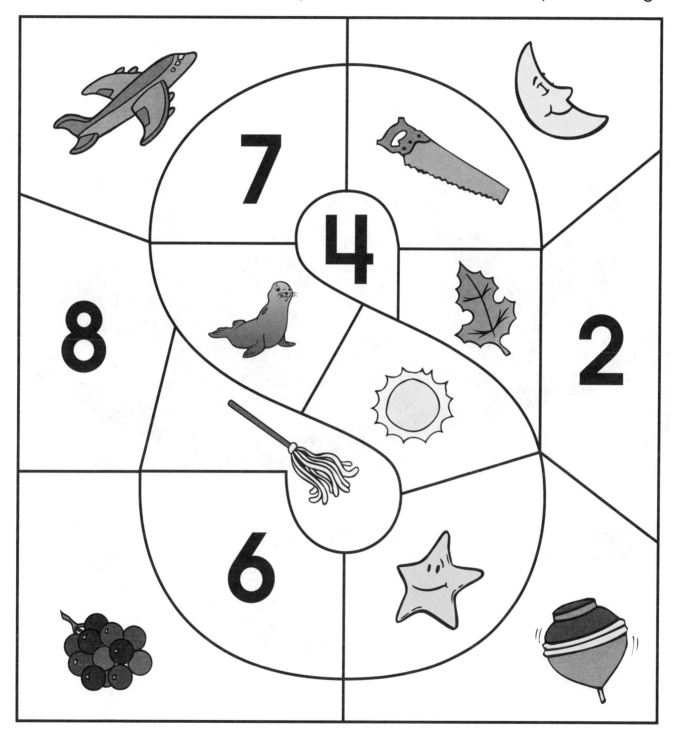

Beginning Consonant Tt

Directions: Say the picture name for each toy in the tub. Draw an **X** on the pictures whose names begin with the same sound as **tub**.

Name _____

Short Vowel Uu

Directions: Short Uu is the sound you hear in the middle of the word **bug**. Help the bug get to the leaf. Follow the path with the pictures whose names have the **short Uu** sound.

Beginning Consonant Vv

Directions: These pictures begin with the letter **Vv**. Color these pictures.

BE MINE

valentine

vase

vacuum

violin

Beginning Consonant Ww

Directions: These pictures begin with the letter **Ww**. Color these pictures.

wagon

watch

watermelon

window

Name _____

Consonant Xx

Directions: Write an **x** on the lines to complete each picture name. Then color the big **X**.

e ___ it   ___ -ray

bo ___   fo ___

Name _____

Beginning Consonant Yy

Directions: Say each picture name. Draw a green line from each ball of yarn to the pictures that begin with the **Yy** sound.

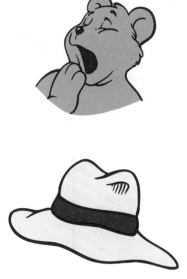

Beginning Consonant Zz

Directions: The word zero begins with the letter **Zz**. Complete the picture of the zero below.

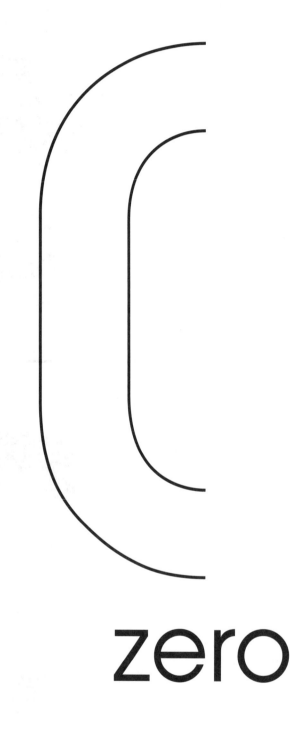

zero

Page 119

Colors

Directions: Draw something that is **red**.

Answers will vary.

Now, trace the word **red**.

red

Page 120

Colors

Directions: Circle the **yellow** picture in each row.

Page 121

Colors

Directions: Draw something that is **blue**.

Answers will vary.

Now, trace the word **blue**.

blue

Page 122

Colors

Directions: Circle the **green** picture in each row.

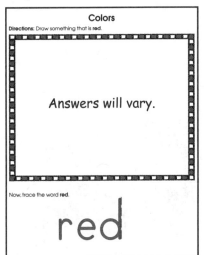

Page 123

Colors

Directions: Draw something that is **orange**.

Answers will vary.

Now, trace the word **orange**.

orange

Page 124

Colors

Directions: In each row, color two things that are the same color.

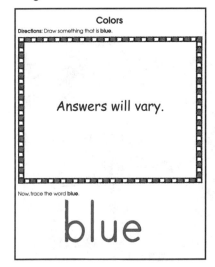

Page 125

Colors

Directions: Draw a line to match each picture to the crayon with the same color.

Page 126

Shapes

Directions: This picture has **circles** in it. Trace the circles.

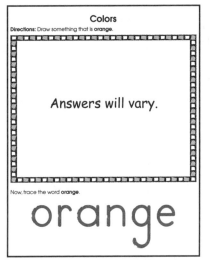

Page 127

Shapes

Directions: This picture has **squares** in it. Trace the squares.

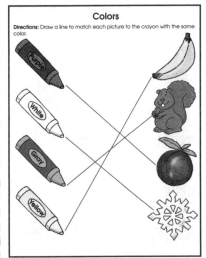

Summer Link Super Edition Grade K

Page 128

Shapes

Directions: This picture has **triangles** in it. Trace the triangles.

Page 129

Shapes

Directions: This picture has **rectangles** in it. Trace the rectangles.

Page 130

Shapes

Directions: This picture has **ovals** in it. Trace the ovals.

Page 131

Shapes

Directions: This picture has a **diamond** in it. Trace the diamond.

Page 132

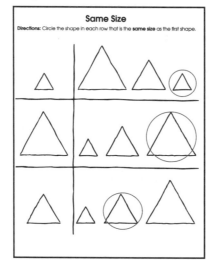

Same Size

Directions: Circle the shape in each row that is the **same size** as the first shape.

Page 133

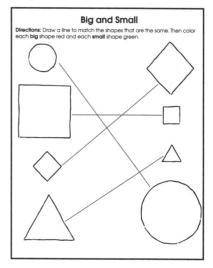

Big and Small

Directions: Draw a line to match the shapes that are the same. Then color each **big** shape red and each **small** shape green.

Page 134

Shorter

Directions: Look at the glass below. Draw another glass beside it. Make your glass **shorter** than the first one.

Page 135

Taller

Directions: Look at the house on the left. Draw a roof on the house beside it. Make the roof on the other house **taller** than the first one.

Page 136

Short and Tall

Directions: Circle each **short** person below. Draw a line under each **tall** person.

Summer Link Super Edition Grade K

Page 137

Long and Short

Directions: Circle each **long** thing. Then draw a line under each **short** thing.

Page 138

Review Size

Directions: Color the **longest** crayon **red**. Color the **shortest** crayon **purple**.

Directions: Circle two bears that are the **same size**.

Page 139

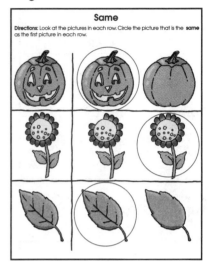

Same

Directions: Look at the pictures in each row. Circle the picture that is the **same** as the first picture in each row.

Page 140

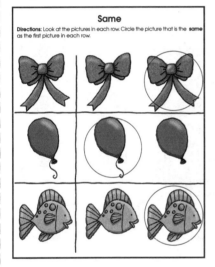

Same

Directions: Look at the pictures in each row. Circle the picture that is the **same** as the first picture in each row.

Page 141

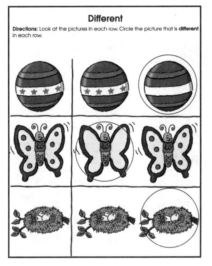

Different

Directions: Look at the pictures in each row. Circle the picture that is **different** in each row.

Page 142

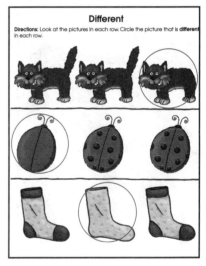

Different

Directions: Look at the pictures in each row. Circle the picture that is **different** in each row.

Page 143

Opposites

Directions: Draw a picture of the opposite.

| day | Night picture |
| sad | Happy face |

Page 144

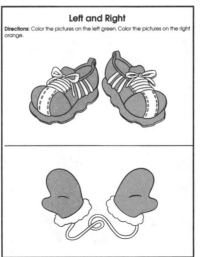

Left and Right

Directions: Color the pictures on the left **green**. Color the pictures on the right **orange**.

Page 149

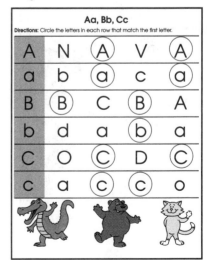

Aa, Bb, Cc

Directions: Circle the letters in each row that match the first letter.

A	N	A	V	A
a	b	a	c	a
B	B	C	B	A
b	d	a	b	a
C	O	C	D	C
c	a	c	c	o

Page 150

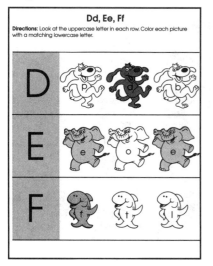

Dd, Ee, Ff

Directions: Look at the uppercase letter in each row. Color each picture with a matching lowercase letter.

Page 151

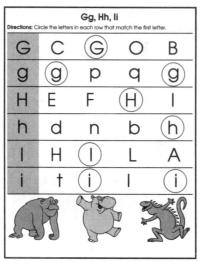

Gg, Hh, Ii

Directions: Circle the letters in each row that match the first letter.

Page 152

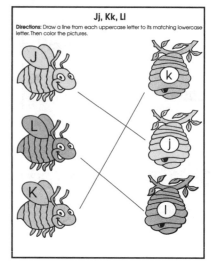

Jj, Kk, Ll

Directions: Draw a line from each uppercase letter to its matching lowercase letter. Then color the pictures.

Page 153

Review Aa–Mm

Directions: Help Adam get to the playground. Follow the letters in ABC order.

Page 154

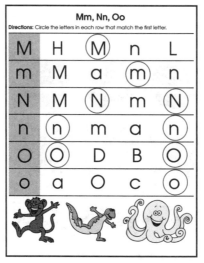

Mm, Nn, Oo

Directions: Circle the letters in each row that match the first letter.

Page 155

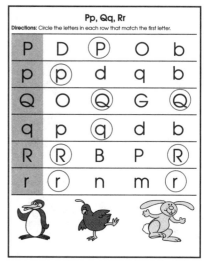

Pp, Qq, Rr

Directions: Circle the letters in each row that match the first letter.

Page 156

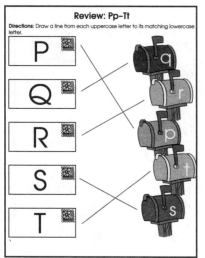

Review: Pp–Tt

Directions: Draw a line from each uppercase letter to its matching lowercase letter.

Page 157

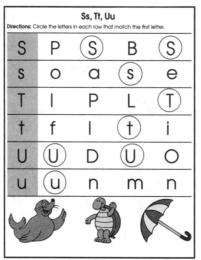

Ss, Tt, Uu

Directions: Circle the letters in each row that match the first letter.

Page 158

Vv, Ww, Xx

Directions: Circle the letters in each row that match the first letter.

Page 159

Yy, Zz

Directions: Circle the letters in each row that match the first letter.

Y	W	(Y)	V	X
y	w	x	v	(y)
Z	N	M	(Z)	W
z	n	(z)	x	m

Page 160

ABC Order

Directions: Connect the dots in ABC order. Color the picture.

Page 161

Left to Right

Directions: Help the bear get to the honey. Follow the arrow to trace a path to the honey.

Directions: Help the cow get to the grass. Follow the arrow to trace a path to the grass.

Page 162

Top to Bottom

Directions: Help the firefighters get to the fire. Trace the lines from top to bottom.

Page 163

Curved Lines

Directions: Trace each ocean wave from left to right. Then draw an ocean wave of your own.

Page 164

Top-to-Bottom Lines

Directions: Start at the top. Follow the arrows to trace the dotted lines.

Page 165

Slanted Lines

Directions: Start at the top. Follow the arrows to trace the dotted lines.

Page 166

Curved Lines

Directions: Start at the dots on the left. Follow the arrows to trace the dotted lines.

Page 167

Circles

Directions: Start at the dots on the left. Follow the arrows to trace the dotted lines.

Summer Link Super Edition Grade K

Page 168

Capital Letters

Directions: Names are special. We use **capital letters** to set them apart from other words. Circle the capital letters in the names below.

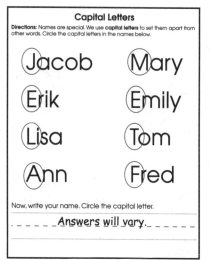

Ⓙacob   Ⓜary

Ⓔrik   Ⓔmily

Ⓛisa   Ⓣom

Ⓐnn   Ⓕred

Now, write your name. Circle the capital letter.

Answers will vary.

Page 169

Capital Letters

Directions: Write your name. Draw a picture of yourself doing something you like.

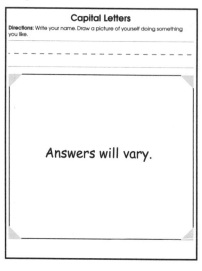

Answers will vary.

Page 170

Writing Your Address

Directions: Write your address. Draw a picture to show where you live.

Answers will vary.

Answers will vary.

Page 171

Short Vowel Aa

Directions: Short **Aa** is the sound at the beginning of the word **alligator**. Color the pictures that begin with the **short Aa** sound.

Page 172

Beginning Consonant Bb

Directions: These pictures begin with the letter **Bb**. Color these pictures.

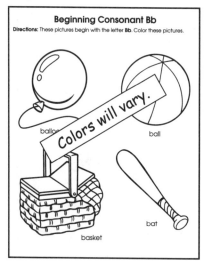

Colors will vary.

balloon   ball   basket   bat

Page 173

Beginning Consonant Cc

Directions: These pictures begin with the letter **Cc**. Color these pictures.

Colors will vary.

coat   cookie   car

Page 174

Beginning Consonant Dd

Directions: Say the picture names in each box on the door. Circle the picture whose name begins with the same sound as **dinosaur**.

Page 175

Short Vowel Ee

Directions: Short **Ee** is the sound in the middle of the word **hen**. Help the hen get to the barn. Follow the path with the pictures whose names have the **short Ee** sound.

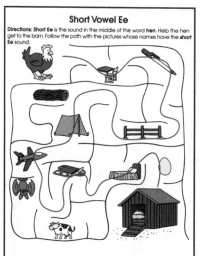

Page 176

Beginning Consonant Ff

Directions: Look at the bubbles below. Say each picture name. If the picture begins with the same sound as **fish**, color it blue.

Page 177

Beginning Consonant Gg

Directions: Say each picture name. Circle the pictures whose names begin with the same sound as **goggles**.

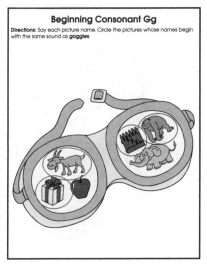

Page 178

Beginning Consonant Hh

Directions: Say each picture name. If the picture begins with the **Hh** sound, color the **hat**.

Page 179

Short Vowel Ii

Directions: Read the words. Draw a line from each word to the picture that matches it.

Page 180

Beginning Sounds Gg, Hh, Ii

Directions: Say the sound the letters make. Circle the pictures in each row that begin with the letter shown.

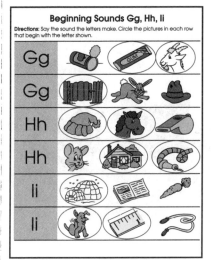

Page 181

Beginning Consonant Jj

Directions: What is Jamie wearing today? Say each picture name. Color the spaces with the **Jj** sound blue. Color the other spaces yellow.

What is Jamie wearing? _____ jeans

Page 182

Beginning Consonant Kk

Directions: Look at the pictures on the kite's tail. Say each picture name. If the picture begins with the same sound as **kite**, color it orange. Then color the kite.

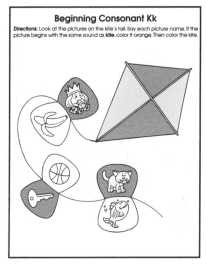

Page 183

Beginning Consonant Ll

Directions: Cut out the stamps at the bottom of the page. Say each picture name. If the picture begins with the same sound as **letter**, glue it on an envelope.

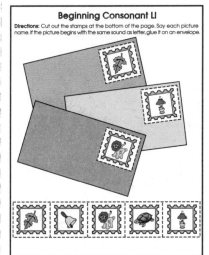

Page 185

Beginning Consonant Mm

Directions: Say each picture name. Color the pictures whose names begin with the same sound as **macaroni** and **meatballs**.

Page 186

Beginning Consonant Nn

Directions: Help the birds find their nest. Follow the path with the pictures whose names begin with the same sound as **nest**.

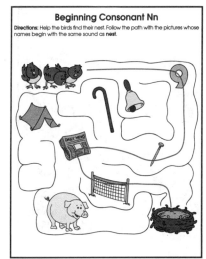

Summer Link Super Edition Grade K

Page 187

Short Vowel Oo

Directions: Write the letter **o** to complete each word. Read the words. Then find the pictures of the words at the bottom of the page and circle them.

fox   log

dog   frog

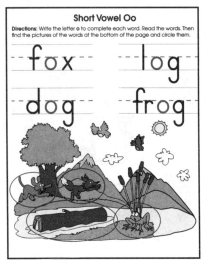

Page 188

Beginning Consonant Pp

Directions: Pam only packs things whose names begin with the same sound as **panda**. Say the picture names. Circle each picture whose name begins with the same sound as **Pam** and **panda**.

Page 189

Beginning Consonant Qq

Directions: Look at the pictures on the quilt below. Say each picture name. If the picture begins with the same sound as **quilt**, color the square yellow. Color the other squares purple.

Page 190

Beginning Consonant Rr

Directions: Who is the raccoon going to visit? Say each picture name. Color the pictures whose names begin with the same sound as **raccoon**.

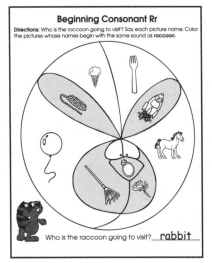

Who is the raccoon going to visit? __rabbit__

Page 191

Beginning Consonant Ss

Directions: Find the letter **S**. Say each picture name. If the picture begins with the same sound as **six**, color the space blue. Color the other spaces orange.

Page 192

Beginning Consonant Tt

Directions: Say the picture name for each toy in the tub. Draw an **X** on the pictures whose names begin with the same sound as **tub**.

Page 193

Short Vowel Uu

Directions: **Short Uu** is the sound you hear in the middle of the word **bug**. Help the bug get to the leaf. Follow the path with the pictures whose names have the **short Uu** sound.

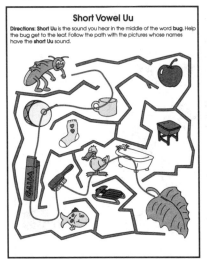

Page 194

Beginning Consonant Vv

Directions: These pictures begin with the letter **Vv**. Color these pictures.

BE MINE

valentine   vase

Colors will vary.

vacuum   violin

Page 195

Beginning Consonant Ww

Directions: These pictures begin with the letter **Ww**. Color these pictures.

wagon   watch

Colors will vary.

watermelon   window

Page 196

Consonant Xx
Directions: Write an **x** on the lines to complete each picture name. Then color the big **X**.

Page 197

Beginning Consonant Yy
Directions: Say each picture name. Draw a green line from each ball of yarn to the pictures that begin with the **Yy** sound.

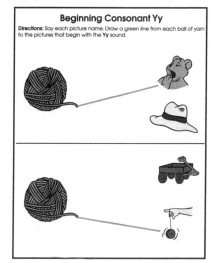

Page 198

Beginning Consonant Zz
Directions: The word zero begins with the letter **Zz**. Complete the picture of the zero below.

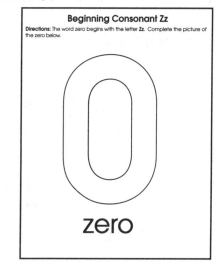

Developmental Skills for Kindergarten Success

Language

Your child

- uses language effectively to express his or her needs and wants and to interact with others.
- can speak in complete sentences.
- asks many questions and looks for answers.
- enjoys being read to and talked to by adults.
- enjoys sharing information about him- or herself and his or her family.
- enjoys language play, nonsense rhymes, songs, riddles, and jokes.
- practices using words and language heard in school.

Cognitive Development

Your child

- has a much longer attention span and can listen to longer, more involved stories.
- can follow multiple-step directions.
- concentrates on tasks from beginning to end.
- can tell left from right.
- can name basic colors and shapes.
- can copy designs and shapes.
- can understand concepts of number, size, position, and time (such as days of the week).
- associates the number of objects with the written numeral.
- can recognize letters and identify the sounds they make.
- is able to print his or her own name.
- can read familiar words.

Developmental Skills for Kindergarten Success

Motor Development

Your child

- can control his or her large muscles. He or she can hop on one foot; jump over objects; and throw, bounce, and catch a ball easily. Your child can also run, climb, skip, tumble, and dance to music.
- is able to dress and clean himself or herself.
- is developing greater control over his or her small muscles. He or she should now be able to tie his or her own shoelaces and manage buttons and zippers.
- can cut on lines and use a paintbrush, crayons, markers, clay, and glue.
- can print uppercase and lowercase letters and his or her name.

Social/Emotional Development

Your child

- is social and enjoys interacting with other children.
- is curious and has an active imagination.
- is confident but still needs praise and encouragement when trying new things.

Reading Notes

Reading Notes

Reading Notes

Reading Notes

Reading Notes

Reading Notes

Reading Notes

Reading Notes

This page intentionally left blank.

KINDERGARTEN SCREENING GUIDE

There is no single quality or skill that enables children to perform well in school. Rather, it's a combination of qualities and skills that contributes to their academic success. Kindergarten readiness screening, which is generally offered in the early spring prior to the start of kindergarten, gives parents and kindergarten staff an inventory of each child's developmental qualities and abilities.

Kindergarten readiness screening provides readiness feedback for parents who want their child to have the best possible start when entering kindergarten. It helps the kindergarten staff get an idea of the developmental level of each child before the year actually begins, so appropriate planning and instruction is in place for the incoming class. At the same time, it provides each child with a low-key, non-threatening opportunity to sample some fun, play-based activities in a comfortable school atmosphere.

Typically, kindergarten staff and other school aides set up several different activity stations in a room for your child to visit. Depending on the size of the staff and the room, the activities may accommodate one child at a time or small groups.

While children participate in the screening activities, parents may be invited to observe silently at a distance so as not to distract or interrupt them. Some screening programs invite parents to complete a Parent Questionnaire at the same time that the screening occurs.

Examples of typical parent questionnaires and activity stations are outlined below.

Parent Questionnaire

Many kindergarten screening programs set up an opportunity for parents to provide their child's medical history and developmental background. Typical questions include:

- complications or special circumstances regarding child's birth, such as a premature delivery
- hospital stays, surgeries, special tests performed
- serious illnesses or injuries
- child's current medications or treatments
- child's current immunization record
- child's early temperament, such as quiet, colicky, carefree, overactive
- child's style of expressing emotion, such as reserved, talkative, temper tantrums
- child's age when developmental milestones, such as speaking first words, were reached
- family information, such as number, age, and sex of child's siblings

Speech, Language, and Hearing Development

It is very important for a child entering kindergarten to be able to understand his or her teachers in order to learn and to know what to do. Likewise, it's very important for a child to be able to speak clearly and to be understood by others in order to express his or her needs. In addition to identifying any speech and hearing disorders, most kindergarten screenings also assess the following language developments:

- speak clearly enough so that people other than child's own family and friends can understand easily
- repeat a simple sentence
- respond to simple directions, such as where to sit, put a book, or throw a ball
- Talk in complete sentences of five to six words
- produce early-developing initial and final consonant sounds—n, m,p,b,h,k,g,f,w,y,t,d
- begin to produce later-developing sounds—s,z,l,r,sh,ch
- look at pictures and then tell stories about them

Self-Help and Social Skills

In kindergarten, young children will need to work well in large groups, get along with new adults and other children, and share the teacher's attention with other youngsters. Classroom routines will also be different from children's at-home routines. Consequently, children need to:

- be able to be away from their parents or people they know for a few hours without being upset.
- be willing and happy to be going to school
- be able to listen attentively when spoken to for three or more minutes
- be willing to try new tasks, and to try them again if they don't succeed the first time
- be able to follow a two- or three-step direction, such as "Close the door and hang up your coat."
- be able to play with other children without having a lot of fights
- be able to do some self-help things for themselves, such as take off and put on jackets and sweaters

Large-Motor Development

Before going to school, children need to have good control over their movements. They need to be able to sit, stand, walk, climb stairs, and run without bumping into things, hurting themselves, or breaking things. In school, they'll be part of a group that is doing the following things:

- walk down steps placing one foot on each step
- walk forward on a line, putting one foot after the other
- walk backwards for six or seven steps without turning to look behind
- stand on one leg at a time for 10 seconds
- stand on two feet, hands on hips, and bend body forward, backward, and sideways
- hop with two feet together
- hop on one foot a few times without falling
- jump using both feet at the same time
- kick a ball
- pump himself or herself on a swing

- balance on one foot for a few seconds
- run without falling frequently
- bounce a ball five consecutive times
- bounce a ball to another person 4 or 5 feet away
- throw and catch a ball using both hands
- carry something on top of something else, such as a juice box on a plate

- touch parts of his or her body with both hands, such as shoulders, neck, knees, toes, hips, chest
- dance while moving forward, backward, sideways left, and sideways right
- skip
- clap hands to music

Small-Motor Development

In school, children need to use their hands and fingers to open and close things and to use things without dropping, breaking, or spilling them. They need to be able to hold pencils and crayons correctly so they can learn to write and do math. Kindergarten screening of the following tasks allows for assessment of small-motor skill development:

- hold a pencil or marker comfortably using thumb and fingers
- open a door using a doorknob
- use crayons without breaking them
- use round-tipped scissors effectively
- color and stay within lines reasonably well
- copy a square on paper
- draw a reasonably good circle on paper
- put together a 9-piece puzzle
- print first name using capital and lowercase letters
- use paste or glue without too much mess
- string wooden beads together
- hammer pegs on a board
- use a spoon without spilling
- get a drink of water without a mess
- turn pages of a book without tearing pages

General Knowledge

Before children start school, there are some things they need to know so they will understand what's going on around them and what teachers and other people are talking about.

- know their own name, age, sex, address or street name, and telephone number
- know mother's and father's first and last names
- know names and ages of brothers and sisters
- name several parts of their own body, such as nose, mouth, hair, eyes, throat, chest, elbow, ankle
- know some things that are around their home, such as bed, door, steps, table
- know some words for when things happen in time, such as now, later, soon, never, before bedtime
- know words for how things compare, such as same, different, more, less
- know something about the places around them and what happens there, such as store, gas station, hospital, doctor's office
- know appropriate words to use to ask to go to the bathroom

Academic Readiness Components

- understands basic concepts
  - positions, such as top, middle, bottom, left, right
  - locations, such as down, up, above, below, across, over
  - quantity, such as less, more, many, few, heavy, light, small, large
  - recognizes feelings, such as happiness, sadness, anger, fear
- demonstrates memory perception
  - knows which object was removed from an earlier group
  - matches objects to pictures
- demonstrates strategies for understanding concepts
  - understands simple cause and effect, such as touching something hot can cause a burn
  - can sort objects into categories, such as vegetables are food
  - can identify and name the capital letters of the alphabet
  - can identify concepts about print, such as recognizing the cover of a book and understanding that words read from left to right
  - understands the difference between letters and numerals
  - can briefly tell a story he or she has just heard
  - can describe what he or she is playing
  - can describe his or her drawing
  - knows some nursery rhymes
  - can state choices about clothing
  - can follow directions for simple games, such as Red Light! Green Light!
  - asks questions beginning with why or how
  - recognizes his or her own name in print
  - makes actual letters, such as those in his or her name
  - attempts to print other letters and some words

Summer Link Super Edition Grade K

Nurture Development

As you help your child get ready for kindergarten, remember that your goal is to nurture excitement for learning. Every skill does not need to be mastered by your child. In fact, complete mastery of every skill by a child is a rarity.

Skills are learned best if they are not turned into lessons. Introduce skills naturally in small doses, reinforcing from time to time through casual conversations and play.

Here are a few tips as you help your child prepare for kindergarten:
- Allow your child to learn by doing.
- Read, read, read, read to your child!
- Envelop your child in language—describe, explain, discover, and communicate at every opportunity.
- Ask your child to describe and explain things of interest.
- Praise your child for asking questions. Asking a question shows a high level of thinking and reasoning.
- Be patient as your child is learning. Don't try too hard or too early. Repetition and practice are helpful when the activity is fun.

Teaching Suggestions

The teaching suggestions on the following pages are a springboard for further learning. Use these activities to spend important time talking and interacting with your child on a daily basis.

Basic Concepts/Skills

• Use color/shape/size words daily when speaking to your child. "The grass is GREEN." "This plate is a CIRCLE." "See the BIG dog."

• Take a color or shape walk with your child. Before you begin, let your child choose between two colors or shapes. Take an object of that color or shape with you on your walk. Ask your child to look for objects that are the same color or shape as the object he/she chose.

• Help your child learn colors, shapes and sizes by making up poems or songs to recite or sing every day.

• From construction paper, cut shapes (squares, ovals, circles, rectangles, triangles, diamonds) and sizes (small, medium, large) from several colors (red, green, blue, yellow, etc.). Have your child sort the shapes according to the category you name.

• Read color, shape and size books with your child. Try the following books, all by Tana Hoban: *Big Ones, Little Ones*; *Circles, Triangles and Squares*; *Colors Everywhere*; *Is It Larger? Is It Smaller?*; *Is It Red? Is It Yellow? Is It Blue?* You might also read *Color* by Christina Rossetti or any version of *The Three Bears*.

- Use a craft knife to cut shape stencils from plastic lids. Have your child use the stencils to create shape pictures.

- Place two similar objects in front of your child. Talk to him/her about how they are the same. Then place two objects that are not alike in front of your child. Talk to him/her about how they are different.

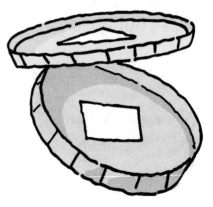

- Using poster board or heavy paper, cut ten cards measuring 12" x 6". Draw a heavy line down the middle of each. Write two sets of letters; one on each side. Make some of the letter cards the same and some different. Turn the cards upside down and have your child find the type of matches you specify—same or different—until all the cards are turned over.

- With your child, look through your pantry or cupboards for food containers that are the same and those that are different. Then set out several pairs of containers, mix them up and have your child match the correct pairs.

- Soak several pairs of cotton balls with different scents (perfumes, scented oils, spices, etc.). Mix up the pairs. Have your child match the scents that smell the same.

Reading Readiness

- Read books and a variety of other things (cereal boxes, food labels, cards, road signs, newspapers, magazines, etc.) with your child daily. Run your finger under the words as you read them, so your child learns that words have meaning and are read from left to right. Let your child see you reading. Take your child to the library and let him/her choose one or two books to read or sign up him/her for story hour.

- Show your child that you value books. Show him/her the proper way to hold a book, to store and put away a book and to turn the pages. Let your child see you handling books with care.

- Read books to your child that contain lots of rhyme and repetition, such as *Mary Wore Her Red Dress* by Merle Peek; *I Went Walking* by Sue Williams; *Brown Bear, Brown Bear, What Do You See?* by Bill Martin, Jr; and *Millions of Cats* by Wanda Gag. The children's librarian at your local library can give you additional suggestions.

- Take your child on a letter hunt when you are outside, in the car or at the grocery store. Find objects that begin with the letters of the alphabet. Invite your child to point out and name the letters he/she finds every day.

Math

- Make three-dimensional number cards with your child. Number index cards 1 through 10. Let your child glue the number of small objects, such as buttons, that correspond to the number on the card.

229

- Using two foam egg cartons, cut out 20 cups. In 10 cups, write the numbers from 1 to 10 on the bottom of the inside of the cup, using a permanent black marker. In the other 10 cups, draw dots that represent the numbers from 1 to 10. Turn over the cups placing the numbers and dots face down, and mix them up. Have your child turn over two cups at a time and try to make matches.

- Using several spoons of various colors, sizes and materials (wood, metal, plastic), ask your child to tell you how all the spoons are different, then how they are alike. Have your child group them into categories, such as by color, size or the material they are made from.

Fine Motor Skills

- Developing fine motor skills is essential for writing readiness. This means working with and manipulating objects with the hands. Working with the hands builds small muscle control needed for writing. You can help your child by providing tools made especially for preschool children: chunky crayons; thick, non-toxic, washable markers; thick, chunky pencils; safety scissors with rounded edges and that are both left- and right-handed; modeling clay; and large beads or pasta for stringing and sorting. Give your child plenty of practice using these tools.

- Make lacing cards by drawing a simple design on a piece of poster board or medium-weight cardboard. Use a hole punch to punch holes along the outside of the design. Cut some yarn, thick string or cord a little longer than you will need to "lace" the picture. Tie a knot in one end of the "thread." Wrap masking tape around the other end to use as a "needle." Help your child lace the yarn through the first one, then let him/her do the next one. Have your child color or decorate the design.

- Give your child spring-type clothespins. Encourage him/her to pick up objects, move them to another place and release them.

- Buy a large notebook for your child to write in. Encourage him/her to draw pictures and write about the pictures. Although your child's first pictures will look like scribbles, these scribbles are an important first stage in writing and will eventually begin to resemble letters and words.

Gross Motor Skills

- Use balls of all sizes to help your child practice throwing, catching and kicking.

- Set up a fitness course, indoors and outdoors, for your child. Have your child help create stations for running; hopping on one foot or skipping around obstacles; walking on tip toe; walking a straight line; jumping over a barrier (no higher than 6"); pedaling a bicycle; or throwing, catching or kicking a ball.

- Fill an old pillowcase with crumpled newspaper and sew the end closed. In an open area in your home, let your child kick the pillowcase around or through objects.

Art

- Encourage your child to express him/herself freely when doing art projects. Avoid asking your child "what" he/she is drawing. Instead, express your interest in your child's work by saying "Tell me about your picture."

- Provide art experiences for your child by taking him/her to an art museum or gallery or check out art books from the library. Ask your child about what he/she likes about a particular work. Ask him/her what he/she thinks may be going on in the work. Avoid going into critical detail about the work. Let your child enjoy the story the artist is telling.

- Keep plenty of art supplies on hand for rainy days or when your child says he/she is bored. Encourage him/her to experiment with several media: painting, collage, print making, sculpture, etc. Also, teach your child that part of being an artist is cleaning up after oneself and putting all supplies back in their proper places.

Cooking

- Cooking can be a rewarding experience for you and your child. Not only are you spending time with and giving your child an important tool for self-care, but you are also teaching your child how to count, measure and cooperate; new words; the importance of following directions; the importance of cleanliness; about time and the order of things; and about textures, colors and shapes.

• Make the cooking experience with your child a total one. Let your child make a picture of ingredients you will need from the grocery store. Let him/her go to the grocery store with you and pick out the ingredients on the list. Have your child help set up the utensils needed, stir, mix, pour and shake; this helps with fine motor skills and hand/eye coordination. Let your child help with cleaning up, too.

Thinking Skills

• Ask your child questions that require him/her to give you more than "yes" or "no" for an answer. For example, "How is applesauce made?"

• Ask your child to repeat a short sentence after you or say one number and ask your child to repeat it. Then ask him/her to repeat two sentences or numbers, then three.

• Make a habit of asking your child to tell you about one or two of his/her favorite activities during the day.

• Show your child a simple picture. Ask him/her to look at it carefully. Take away the picture and ask your child to tell you all the things he/she remembers about the picture.

Kindergarten Readiness Games

Preschoolers are constantly making connections between what they know and what they have just learned. Fun and inviting play-based experiences are the most effective way to develop these connections.

The games and activities that follow offer creative, enriching opportunities to practice kindergarten-readiness skills such as language, literacy, math, and fine-motor development

- Beginning Sound Memory
- Alphabet Word Box
- ABC Fingerplays
- Critical Thinking
- Math Attractions
- Number Match
- Imagination Play
- Self and Environment

Beginning Sound Memory Game

Cut out the letters and pictures below and on pages 237–241.Mix them up and turn them over to match the beginning sound with its picture.

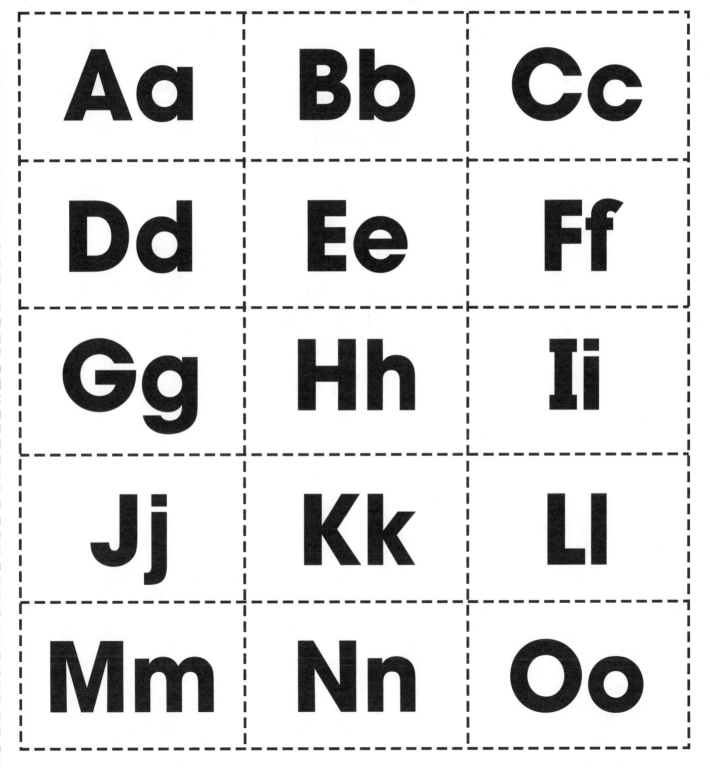

This page was left intentionally
blank for cutting activity on
previous page.

Beginning Sound Memory Game

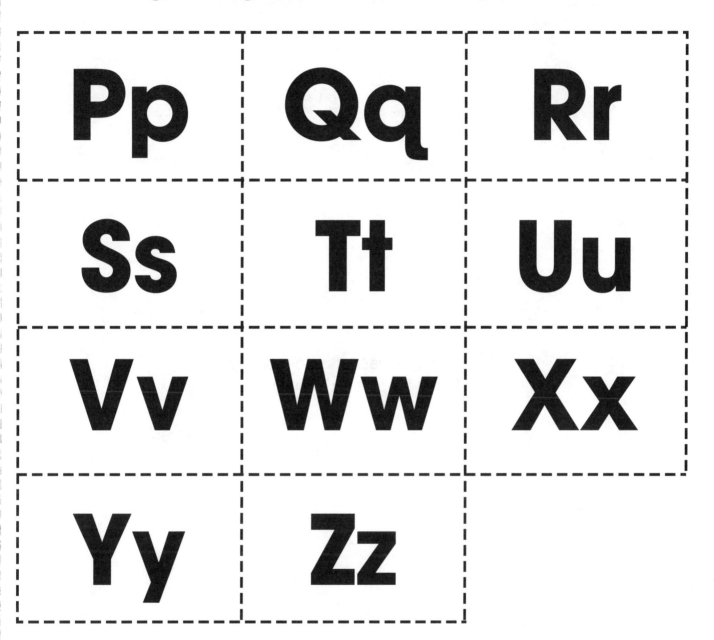

Pp	Qq	Rr
Ss	Tt	Uu
Vv	Ww	Xx
Yy	Zz	

This page was left intentionally
blank for cutting activity on
previous page.

Beginning Sound Memory Game

This page was left intentionally
blank for cutting activity on
previous page.

Beginning Sound Memory Game

Summer Link Super Edition Grade K

This page was left intentionally
blank for cutting activity on
previous page.

Alphabet Word Box

To encourage your preschooler's vocabulary development and awareness of beginning sounds, try playing this game. Choose a letter from the alphabet and place the items or pictures of the items from the list below in a box. Take one item at a time out of the box and have your child tell you what it is.

A

airplane	accordion	arm
alphabet	ant	address
ambulance	apron	animal
arrow	apple	alligator

B

baby	bear	bird	boat
banana	ball	bat	bubble
boy	bus	birthday	balloon
book	button	box	boot

C

car	cow	comb	cat
costume	camel	cookie	cake
cup	candy	coffee	candle
camera	caterpillar	card	cap

D

day	dime	dish	dog
doctor	door	diamond	date
doughnut	daisy	duck	dinosaur
dolphin	deer	daughter	doe

Alphabet Word Box

E

ear	eraser	earth	eight
elf	envelope	elephant	eagle
eleven	eel	easel	eyes
elbow	egg	Eskimo	exit (sign)

F

fish	fox	frog	fire
farm	four	five	face
foot	fan	father	furniture
fig	felt	finger	family

G

giraffe	game	goose	goat
gate	garden	gold	gift
gum	guitar	garbage	grass

H

heart	hair	hand	hammer
horn	helicopter	horse	house
hen	head	hog	hat
hippopotamus	happy	ham	hive

I

invitation	igloo	ice	infant
iguana	ice cream	iron	instrument
inch	insect	island	ivy

Alphabet Word Box

J

jelly or jam   jet   jeans   juice

jello   jacks   jar   jockey

jug   journal   jaws   jewel

K

kite   kaleidoscope   kitchen   kazoo

kitten   king   key   koala

kangaroo   Kleenex   kid   kiss

L

lion   lemon   letter   leg

lime   lamb   lamp   lasso

lollipop   llama   lumber   log

leaf   lace   lily   lake

M

mouse   milk   mittens   mask

man   magnet   machine   mouth

money   monkey   moon   marble

mail   moose   mom   map

N

number   net   night   nest

needle   noodle   necklace   nickel

nail   napkin   newspaper   nurse

neck   nose   nine   nut

Alphabet Word Box

O

owl ostrich oak leaf Olympics
oval octagon oven organ
orange olive oar oatmeal
officer operation orchestra octopus

P–Q

pig purse pencil penny
puppet park police piano
penquin paper perfume pocket
quart queen quilt quarter
Q-tip quartz quail question

R

red rocket rainbow robin
rooster rose ring rug
rake rock rabbit rectangle
raspberry raisin radio raccoon
rat reindeer rhinoceros refrigerator

S

sun sail seal seed
saddle seesaw sea soup
sand Santa soap saw
sock salt sailboat sink

Alphabet Word Box

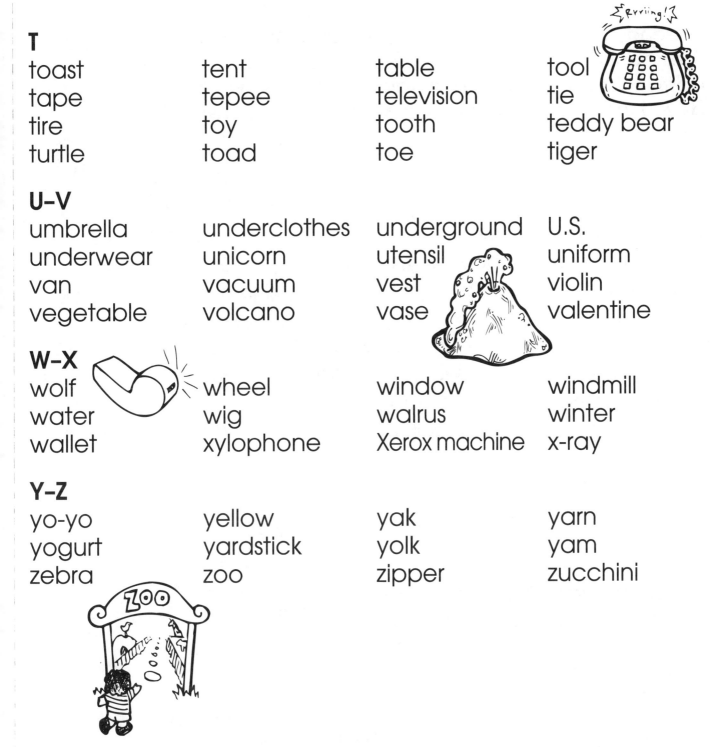

T

toast	tent	table	tool
tape	tepee	television	tie
tire	toy	tooth	teddy bear
turtle	toad	toe	tiger

U–V

umbrella	underclothes	underground	U.S.
underwear	unicorn	utensil	uniform
van	vacuum	vest	violin
vegetable	volcano	vase	valentine

W–X

wolf	wheel	window	windmill
water	wig	walrus	winter
wallet	xylophone	Xerox machine	x-ray

Y–Z

yo-yo	yellow	yak	yarn
yogurt	yardstick	yolk	yam
zebra	zoo	zipper	zucchini

Summer Link Super Edition Grade K

ABC Fingerplays

Preschoolers enjoy the rhythmic predictability of rhyming language. Their ability to see patterns in word sounds will greatly influence their ability to read later on. Encourage your child to mimic your actions as you follow the fingerplay prompts with each rhyme below.

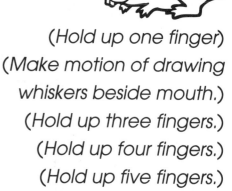

A – Animal Adventures

One little mouse, squeakety, squeak!   (*Hold up one finger*)
Two little kittens, peekety, peek.   (*Make motion of drawing whiskers beside mouth.*)

Three little puppies, bow-wow-wow!   (*Hold up three fingers.*)
Four little roosters, cock-a-doodle-doo!   (*Hold up four fingers.*)
Five old hens, clack clack clack!   (*Hold up five fingers.*)
Six fat ducks, quack, quack, quack.   (*Hold up six fingers.*)

B – Bobby

Bobby's fingers, Bobby's nose,
Bobby's head, Bobby's toes.
Bobby's ears, Bobby's eyes,
Bobby's arms, Bobby's thighs.
Bobby's neck, Bobby's cheeks,
Bobby's shoulders, Bobby peeks.
Bobby's mouth, Bobby's hips,
Bobby's thumbs, and Bobby's lips.

    (*Replace Bobby's name with your child's name, and point to each body part mentioned while you say this rhyme.*)

C – Cats Asleep

When all of my cats are asleep in the sun,
I like to count them one by one.
The first is Candy so cunning and sweet.
   (point to each of four fingers.)
The second is Captain who looks so neat.
The third is Cotton with cuddly fur.
The fourth is Cubby with happy purr.
When all of my cats are asleep in the sun,
I like to count them one by one.
   (Ask your child to name the fifth, sixth, seventh, eighth, etc., cats.)

D – Five Young Ducks

Five young ducks went out to play
Over the hills and far away.
Mother duck called them,
"Quack, quack, quack."
But only four little ducks came waddling back.
(Continue the rhyme until no ducks return. End the rhyme with;)
Old Mother Duck went out one day
Over the hills and far away.
She called all her babies,
"Quack, quack, quack."
And all five little ducks came waddling back.

E – Elephants

One little elephant was playing in the sun.
He thought that playing was such a lot of fun,
He called another elephant and asked him to come.
Two little elephants were playing in the sun.
They thought that playing was such a lot of fun,
They called another elephant and asked her to come.
Ten little elephants were playing in the sun.
They thought that playing was such a lot of fun,
They didn't call another elephant to come.

F – What the Fingers Said

The fingers went to walk one day,
And this is what I heard them say:
Thumb said, "I am fat, you see,
But no one ever laughs at me."
Pointer said this with a shout,
"Folks need me to point things out!"
Middle said, "I'm very long,
But I keep the others strong."
Ring said, "Important I must be
When someone puts a ring on me."
Little one said, "Oh, please don't fuss.
_____ needs all of us!"

(Point to one finger at a time, and substitute your child's name each time the rhyme is said.)

G – Grandmother's Spectacles

Here are Grandmother's Spectacles,
(Make circles around eyes with thumbs and pointer fingers.)
Here is Grandfather's hat.
(Hold both hands as a hat over head.)
I lay my hands on my lap,
Just like that!
(Fold hands in lap.)

H – Hippopotamus

This hippopotamus looks like a hog.
This hippopotamus is a very large size.
This hippopotamus weighs 8000 pounds.
This hippopotamus has very small eyes.
This hippopotamus has bristles on his head.

I – If You Can

If you can stand on the tips of your toes,   *(Stand on tiptoes.)*
I will give you a red, red rose.   *(Hold up one finger.)*
If you can stand way back on your heels,   *(Stand on heels.)*
I will give you two orange peels.   *(Hold up two fingers.)*
If you can bend down and touch the floor,   *(Bend and touch floor)*
I will give you three apple cores.   *(Hold up three fingers.)*
If you can twist to the left and the right,   *(Twist to left and right.)*
I will give you four candy bites.   *(Hold up four fingers.)*
If you can reach your hands to the sky,   *(Reach hands up.)*
I will give you five pieces of pie.   *(Hold up five fingers.)*
I wish that this game was not pretend,
And I am sorry that it has to end.

(Ask your child what other things can be done with his or her fingers, hands, and body.)

J – Jumping Jack

I am a little jumping jack.
I jump out of my box and I jump right back.
I jump up high, I bend down low,
For that is the way that I must go.
I jump to the left, I jump to the right,
I jump in my box and I hide out of sight.
I jump up and down and I turn all around,
And I jump right out and land on the ground.

(Secure a large empty box that will hold your child comfortably and let your child pretend to be the jumping jack.)

K - Kangaroo

Old hoppity-loppity kangaroo
Can jump much faster than I or you.
　　　Hoppity-loppity, jump, one-two　　　　　*(Child jumps.)*
Her tail is bent like a kitchen chair.
So she can sit down while she combs her hair.
　　　Hoppity-loppity, jump, one-two　　　　　*(Child jumps.)*
She has a pouch where her baby grows.
She carries the baby wherever she goes.
　　　Hoppity-loppity, jump, one-two　　　　　*(Child jumps.)*
And when she jumps, she uses her tail,
So she can jump farther and almost sail.
　　　Hoppity-loppity, jump, one-two.　　　　　*(Child jumps.)*
　　(Give two long jumps, one short jump on the words "hoppity-loppity, jump," and two quick jumps on the count "one-two.")

L - Ladybugs

Tick-tack-tick-tack! See them go!
Four little ladybugs are marching in a row.
　　(Hold up four fingers.)
The first one is yellow
　　　and trimmed with specks of black.
　　(Point to one finger at a time.)

The second one is orange with a round and shiny back.
The third one is bright red with teeny, tiny dots.
The fourth one is fancy with different kinds of spots.
Ladybugs help ranchers. Ladybugs have use.
They eat up all the tree pests,
So we can have orange juice!
　　(To make a ladybug, have your child paint the back of a small paper plate red. When the paint is dry, add a small half-circle head and dots made from black construction paper. Then attach six legs made from black pipe cleaners.)

M – One Old Man Went Out to Mow

One old man went out to mow,
Went out to mow in the meadow.
Two old men went out to mow,
Went out to mow in the meadow.
Two old men and one old man
Went out to mow in the meadow.
Three old men went out to mow,
Went out to mow in the meadow.
Three old men and two old men and one old man
Went out to mow in the meadow.
   (Point to one finger at a time.)

N – Nap Time

One little puppy jumps in my lap.
He takes a nap in Daddy's cap.
One little kitten purrs a tune.
She takes a nap every afternoon.
One little boy/girl with curly head
Knows it is time to go to bed.
   (Point to one finger at a time.)

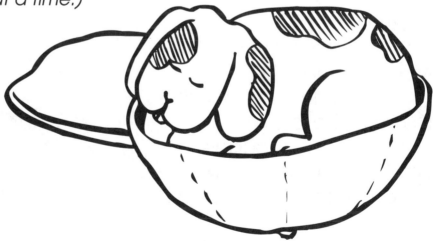

O – Octopus, Octopus

Octopus, octopus down by the sea.
How many arms can you show to me?
Only one, or will it be two?
   (Show one finger, then two.)
Why are all of these arms on you?
Will it be three or will it be four?
   (Show three fingers, then four.)
Oh, dear me! Are there really more?
Will it be five or will it be six?
   (Show five fingers, then six.)
I think that my eyes are playing tricks.
Will it be seven or will it be eight?
   (Show seven fingers, then eight.)
Tell me octopus. I cannot wait.
Octopus, octopus down by the sea,
How many arms can you show me?
Child: "I have eight arms, as you can see."
   (Show eight fingers.)
   (Create an octopus by painting a paper bag gray. Stuff it with newspaper and tie it at the "neck." Add eight streamers for arms.)

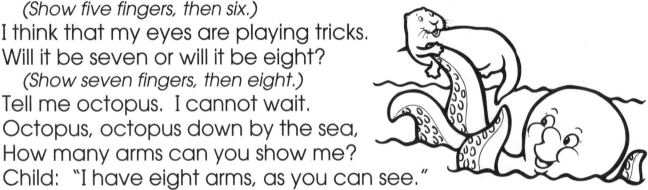

P – Puddle

One puddle, two puddles
Made by the rain.
Three puddles, four puddles
Down in the lane.
Five puddles, six puddles
We can wade through.
Seven puddles, eight puddles
Quite muddy, too!
Nine puddles, ten puddles
Covering tiny roots.
Eleven puddles, twelve puddles—
We all need our boots.

SH-H-H-H!

Q - Quiet Time

Be quiet, feet.
Be quiet, legs.
Be a hen sitting on eggs.
Be quiet, fingers.
Be quiet, wrists.
Let your hands make tiny fists.
Be quiet, shoulders.
Be quiet, chest.
Be a bird asleep in a nest.

(Ask, "What other parts of your body do you want to be quiet? Show me how a bird sleeps in a nest.")

R - I Can Raise My Right Hand

I can raise my right hand.
    I can raise it high.
I can wave my right hand.
    At an airplane in the sky.
I can raise my left hand.
    I can raise it high.
I can wave my left hand
    At an airplane in the sky.

(Before beginning the poem, ask your child to demonstrate raising his or her left and right hands.)

S – Ten White Seagulls

Ten white seagulls   (Hold up ten fingers.)
Just see them fly   (Make motion of flying.)
Over the mountain,
And up to the sky.   (Raise arms high.)
Ten white seagulls   (Hold up ten fingers.)
Crying aloud,
Spread out their wings,
And fly over a cloud.   (Make motion of flying.)
Ten white seagulls   (Hold up ten fingers.)
On a bright day.
Pretty white seagulls,
Fly, fly away!   (Pretend to fly around the room.)

T – Tiptoeing

I tiptoe here and I tiptoe there.
I tiptoe as lightly as wings in the air.
I tiptoe along in my two little shoes.
I tiptoe softly as a kitten mews.
I tiptoe slowly with no rush.
I tiptoe quietly as a hush.
I tiptoe here and I tiptoe there.
And tiptoe over to sit in my chair.
   (Have your child tiptoe around the room as you say the rhyme.)

U – Umbrellas

I put on my raincoat.
I put on my hat.
I put up my umbrella
Just like that!
Umbrellas go up,
Umbrellas go down,
When the rain clouds are dark
All over the town.

V — Valentines

I'll send you one valentine, that's what I'll do.
I'll send you one valentine, and maybe two!
I'll send you two valentines, wait and see.
I'll send you two valentines, and maybe three!
I'll send you three valentines from the best store.
I'll send you three valentines, I cannot do more!
I'll send you four valentines, that's all I can do.
But on each one I will write: "I love you."

W — Wiggles

A wiggle-wiggle here,
A wiggle-wiggle there.
Wiggle you hands up in the air.
Wiggle your shoulders
Wiggle your hips
Wiggle your knees
And move your lips
Wiggle, wiggle, wiggle,
And wiggle some more;
Now let's sit down on the floor.

X — The Xylophone

Grandpa and I went to hear play
musical sounds only yesterday.
A rum-ba-bum-bum, so said the drum.
A song by the oboe came after the cello.
From the back was born, a cry from the horn.
A root-a-toot-toot echoed the flute.
I realized I'd slept, while the violin wept.
Grandpa gave me a poke, and suddenly I woke
to hear sounds that I swear had a beauty so rare
That I wanted to stay and learn how to play
the instrument that made so lovely a tone—
None other than—the amazing xylophone.

Y — Yawns

I saw a puppy yawn and yawn!
I caught the yawns and then
I yawned, and yawned, and yawned–ho hum!
And then I yawned again.
I saw my kitten yawning.
I had to stop and play.
I yawned at least one minute
And yawned the yawns away.
The animals make me sleepy,
With mouths so yawning wide.
I must relax and close my eyes.
I feel so many yawns inside.

Z — Counting at the Zoo

Count one: 1.
Come and have some fun!
Count two: 1, 2.
Let's run to the zoo!
Count three: 1, 2, 3.
A monkey's in the tree.
Count four: 1, 2, 3, 4.
Hear the animals roar!
Count five: 1, 2, 3, 4, 5.
Watch the porpoise dive.
Count six: 1, 2, 3, 4, 5, 6.
An ape is doing tricks.
Count seven: 1, 2, 3, 4, 5, 6, 7.
The giraffe is as high as heaven.

Critical Thinking

Let your child color and cut apart the cards below. Then have him or her put the cards in the correct order. Fasten them together to make a book.

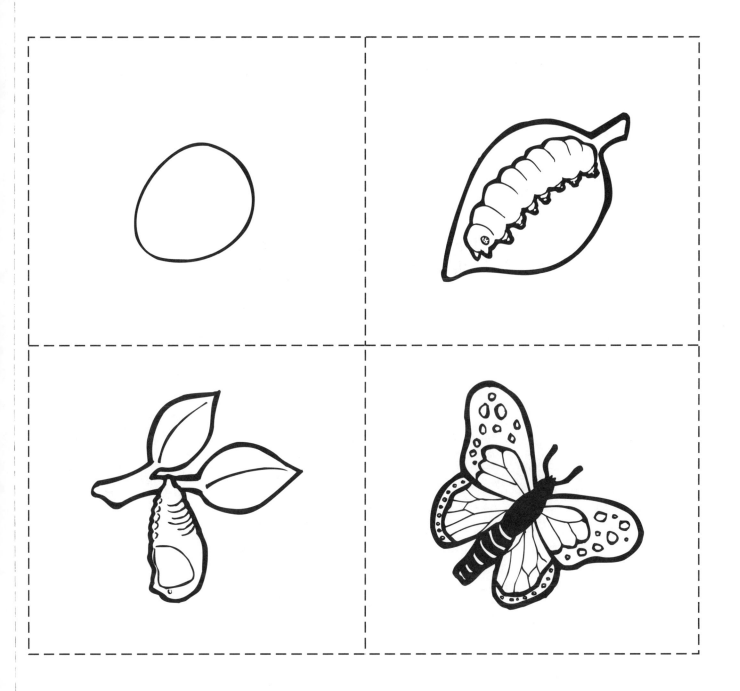

This page was left intentionally
blank for cutting activity on
previous page.

Critical Thinking

Let your child color and cut apart the cards below. Then have him or her put the cards in a straight line according to size.

Summer Link Super Edition Grade K

This page was left intentionally
blank for cutting activity on
previous page.

Critical Thinking

Let your child color and cut apart the cards below. Then have him or her put the cards in the correct order. Fasten them together to make a book.

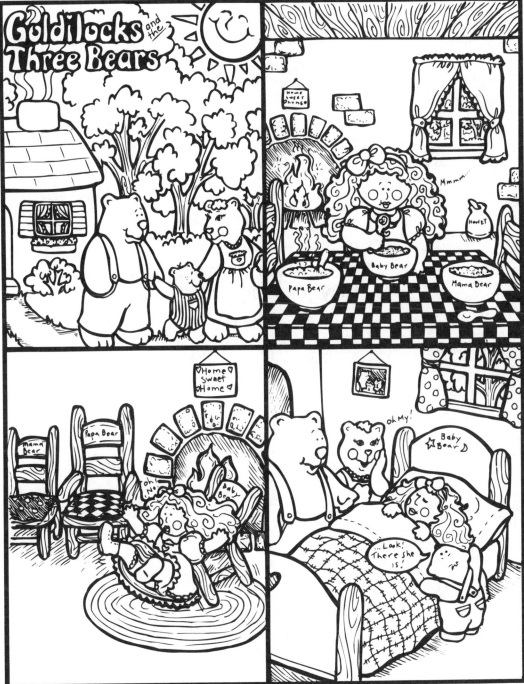

This page was left intentionally
blank for cutting activity on
previous page.

Critical Thinking

Let your child color and cut apart the cards below. Then have him or her put the cards in the correct order. Fasten them together to make a book.

This page was left intentionally
blank for cutting activity on
previous page.

Critical Thinking

Let your child draw and color details on the trees below according to each season of the year. Then have him or her cut the cards apart and put them in correct order. Fasten them together to make a book.

SUMMER

AUTUMN

WINTER

SPRING

This page was left intentionally
blank for cutting activity on
previous page.

Critical Thinking

Let your child color and cut apart the pattern pieces for the clown puppet. Have him or her glue the puppet face to the bottom of a lunch-sized paper bag. Fold the bottom down to flatten the bag. Then ask your child to position and glue the neck ruffle piece slightly lower than the face and under the flattened-bottom fold.

This page was left intentionally
blank for cutting activity on
previous page.

Critical Thinking

Color and cut apart the cards below. Ask your child to match each mother to its baby.

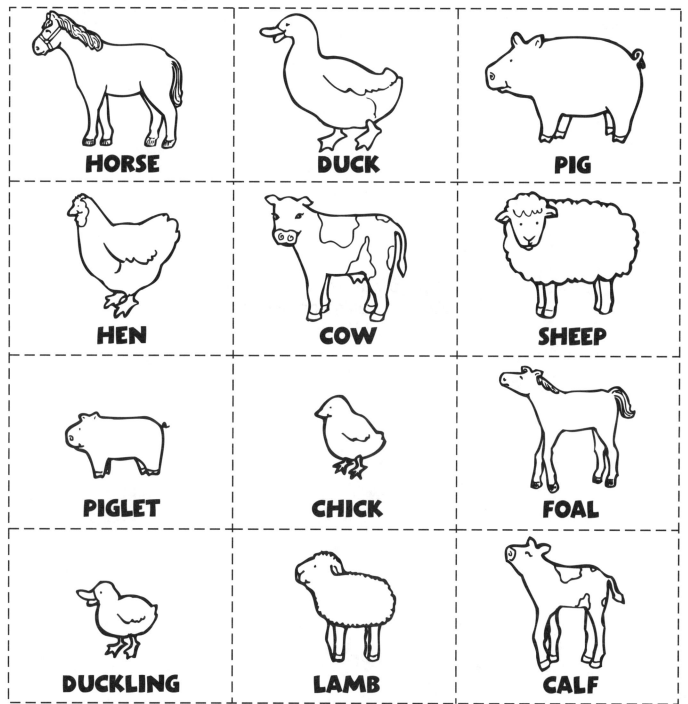

HORSE **DUCK** **PIG**

HEN **COW** **SHEEP**

PIGLET **CHICK** **FOAL**

DUCKLING **LAMB** **CALF**

This page was left intentionally
blank for cutting activity on
previous page.

Critical Thinking

Draw a line from each animal to its shadow.

Math Attractions

The following play activities allow your preschooler to discover and develop early math concepts while simply having fun.

Abra-ca-dabra

Place several objects on a table. Let your child look at the objects and count them quickly. Place a box in front of the objects so your child can no longer see them. Remove some of the objects. Show your child the objects again. Ask him or her to figure out how many objects are missing. This is a fun "magical" game to use when you want to introduce the concept of subtraction. Even very young preschoolers are able to understand that a certain number of objects are gone.

Bingo

Bingo is a wonderful game to help children learn to recognize numbers. Print numbers 1 through 9 in random order on a nine-square grid. Your child wins when he or she covers three numbers in a row. This game is also fun to create using shapes or sets of objects. The possibilities are endless!

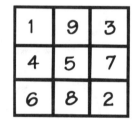

Clocks

Clocks are wonderful for simply learning how to identify numbers and to begin the concept of telling time. Make paper plate clocks that have the time set for activities that always happen at the same time each day (lunch, snack, naps, etc.). Show your child that the times of the "real" clock match the paper plate clocks. They can set their clocks for "bedtime" or "getting-up-in-the-morning" time.

Copy Cat

Make clapping sounds and invite your child to imitate the pattern. Add slapping sounds so that the pattern becomes clap, slap. Vary the number of times each sound is made. Then add foot-tapping sounds. The pattern then becomes clap, slap, tap. Snapping fingers can also be added. Vary the order of the sounds to form new patterns: clap, clap, slap, clap, tap, tap, snap, tap. Have your child repeat the patterns.

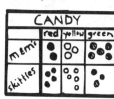

Graphing Activities

Graphing activities teach your child important early math concepts, such as one-to-one correspondence and classifying. Invite your child to graph the number of different colors in a bag of M&Ms, or the number of friends who have pets versus friends who don't, or the number of vegetables versus fruits in your refrigerator.

Height Chart

Purchase or make a growth chart to hang on a wall in your home. Record the heights of your child and several friends. Children love to actually "see" how much they are growing. Using the information provided on the height chart, ask, "Who is the tallest? Shortest? Same height?" Then organize the children by seriation (tallest to shortest or vice versa).

I Guess

Fill a small jar with jelly beans. Ask your child to guess (estimate) how many jelly beans are in the jar. After he or she has guessed, count the jelly beans aloud together. When the counting is done, divide the jelly beans equally among your child and his or her friends. You can increase the difficulty of this activity by using baby food jars. Fill several baby food jars with jelly beans. After counting the number of jelly beans in the first jar, ask your child if one jar has "more" or "less than" the previous jar.

Jump Rope

Jumping rope is a wonderful way to teach rote counting, counting by twos, fives, or tens. Here are two counting rhymes you can use when your child jumps rope:

1. (Insert name) likes to jump. (Insert name) likes to count. (Insert name) knows her numbers. Listen as she counts. (Then count by 1's, 2's, 5's, or 10's as your child jumps.)

2. Going to the market. Going to the store. We need some treats. How many more? (Then count by 1's, 2's, 5's, or 10's as your child jumps.)

Measure Up

Many tools that measure things have numbers and lines. Show your child the following items and ask what each tool would measure: measuring cups, measuring spoons, thermometer, tape measure, ruler, calendar, clock.

Mystery Numerals

Moisten the end of a cotton swab. Lightly print a numeral in the palm of your child's hand. Can your child guess which numeral you made?

Sorting Extravaganza

Have your child:

- Sort objects by color (pegs, buttons, toys, cards).
- Sort objects by shape (parquetry, blocks, beans, beads).
- Sort food by taste (sweet, salty, bitter, spicy, sour).
- Sort sounds as loud or soft.
- Sort toys by where they belong in the classroom.
- Sort clothes by type (shirt, dress, pants, blouse, socks).
- Sort objects by what they are made from (glass, metal, wood, plastic).
- Sort objects by function (screwdriver, hammer, mixer, table, chair, rake).

What Is Missing?

Place three to six shapes in front of your child. Ask him or her to name the shapes. Then tell your child to close his or her eyes or to look away. Remove one of the shapes, and ask your child which shape is missing.

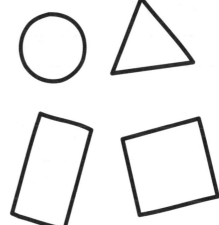

Practice Writing Numbers

1 2 3 4 5 6 7 8 9 10

Number Match Game

Cut out the cards below and on pages 281 to 289. Then match the number cards with the cards that have the same number of dots.

This page was left intentionally
blank for cutting activity on
previous page.

Number Match Game

This page was left intentionally
blank for cutting activity on
previous page.

Number Match Game

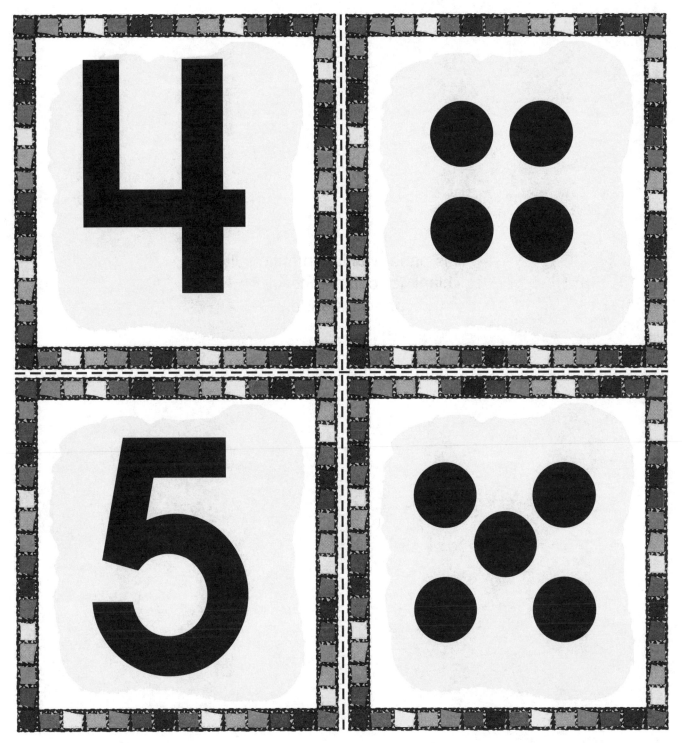

This page was left intentionally
blank for cutting activity on
previous page.

Name _____

Number Match Game

This page was left intentionally
blank for cutting activity on
previous page.

Number Match Game

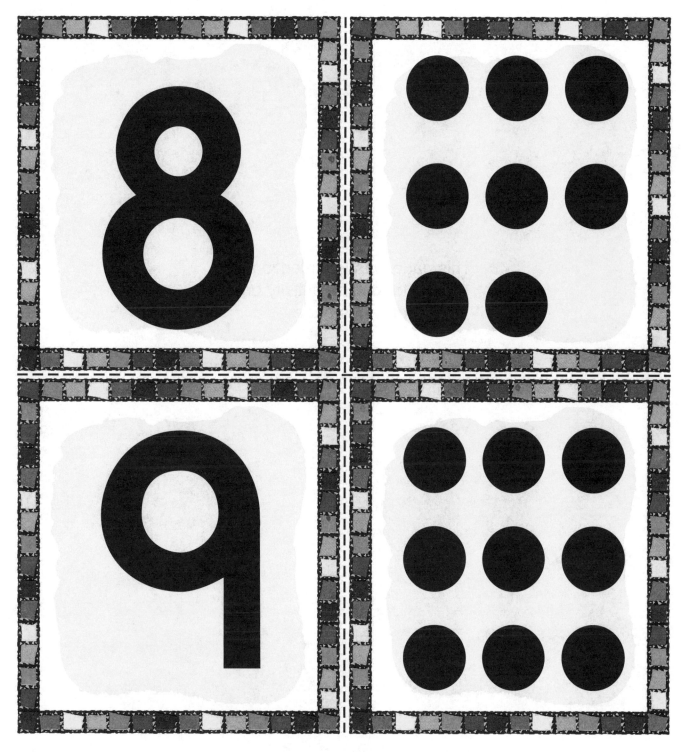

This page was left intentionally
blank for cutting activity on
previous page.

Number Match Game

This page was left intentionally
blank for cutting activity on
previous page.

Imagination Play

Airplane

Play Props: suitcases, small pillows, blankets, food trays, magazines, pens, paper, dishes

Setting: chairs, cockpit window, counter for ticket agent, headsets, instrument panel, microphone, plane seats, steering wheel

Costumes: Pilot hats, scarves, ties, vests, dress-up clothes

Play Possibilities:
- Passengers can get ready for a trip by packing suitcases, dress up in travel clothes, go to the airport, purchase tickets, sit in the waiting area, board the plane, or eat a meal on board.
- Agents can sell tickets or assign seats.
- Flight attendants can show passengers to their seats, serve drinks and meals, and give safety instructions.
- The ground crew can load the plane with baggage, direct the plane to move, and unload the plane after it lands.

Restaurant

Play Props: dishes, utensils, coffee pot, water pitcher, pots and pans, cooking utensils, imaginary food, order pads, pencils

Setting: tables, tablecloths, chairs, cash register, play money, menus, toy sink and stove, coat tree, restaurant sign

Costumes: aprons, chef hats, dress-up clothes

Play Possibilities:
- Customers can order from the menu, enjoy eating the food, practice using good manners, and pay the bill.
- Chefs can prepare the food.
- Waiters and waitresses can take orders, serve food, and set and clear the table.
- Host or hostess seats customers, provides menus, receives money, and makes change.

Fire Station

Play Props: garden hose or hose from an old vacuum cleaner, ladder, bucket, sponges, map of a city, paper and pencils, telephone

Setting: fire engine, countertop, tables

Costumes: yellow slickers, black rubber boots, fire fighter hats

Play Possibilities:
- Fire fighters can wear slickers, boots, and hats. They can ride the engine, make a siren noise, use the hose to put out a pretend fire, return to the fire station, clean the fire truck, and finally, hang up the hose to dry.
- Dispatchers can take phone calls about fires. They can rescue cats from trees, or they might help call the ambulance for injured people.

Flower Shop

Play Props: real or fake flowers, tissue paper, stapler, ribbon, pad of paper, pencil, telephone, delivery truck, a variety of containers such as vases or pots

Setting: flower shop sign, work and display tables, countertop, shelves, cash register, play money

Costumes: smocks or aprons, dress-up clothes

Play Possibilities:
- Flower shop clerks can design flower arrangements for display, write up orders, deliver arrangements, receive payments, and make change.
- Customers can dress up in the home area and go out shopping for arrangements to decorate the home, pay for the arrangements at the flower shop, find a place to display the flowers attractively, and finally, enjoy looking and smelling them.

Grocery Store

Play Props: toy shopping carts, fruits and vegetables, plastic eggs and cartons, empty food boxes, empty plastic bottles, cans, paper, pencils, paper bags

Setting: shelves, countertop, cash register, play money, price signs, grocery store sign

Costumes: aprons and shirts

Play Possibilities:
- Customers can make shopping lists, push shopping carts, and choose, pay for, and take home groceries.
- Clerks can stock shelves and help customers find what they need.
- Checkers can ring up sales, take money, and make change.
- Baggers pack the customer's groceries and carry them to his or her car.

School

Play Props: alphabet cards, pencils, rulers, lined and unlined paper, crayons, readers and other books, dot-to-dot books, number games, large clock, dolls

Dramatic Setting: tables, desks, chairs, shelves, a blackboard if possible

Costumes: one child is dressed like a teacher, the others in normal play clothing

Play Possibilities:

- Teachers can teach dolls, stuffed animals, or other children. They can direct activities, decide on tasks, lead a reading group, or assign writing projects.
- Students can do writing projects, copy the alphabet, or do small number games.

Self and Environment

The following activities allow preschoolers to develop a sense of who they are and to express their feelings about their environment.

Have your child draw and color his or her face in the mirror below.

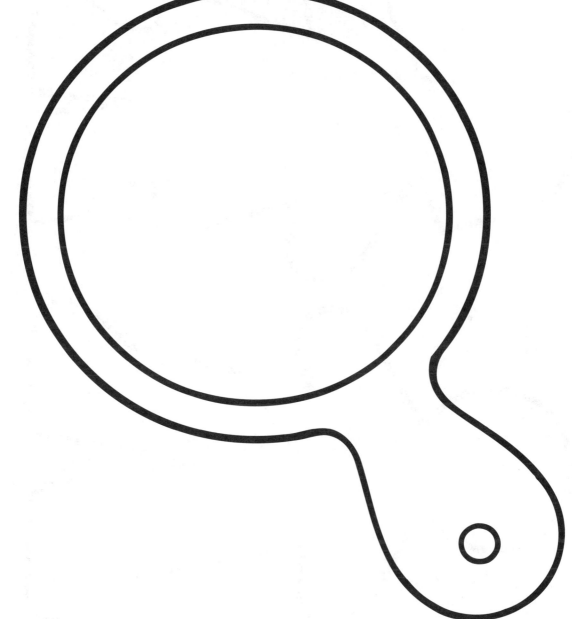

Self and Environment

Invite your child to draw and color features for the boy and girl outlines below. Encourage using as many facial and clothing details as he or she can think of to personalize them.

Self and Environment

Invite your child to draw and color things that might appear in the rooms of the house below.

Self and Environment

Invite your child to draw and color his or her favorite foods and beverage in the picture below.

Name _____

Self and Environment

Invite your child to identify the four moods that are shown in the pictures below. Ask your him or her to tell you about a time when he or she experienced each of those feelings. Then have your child cut apart the pictures and fasten them into a book.

This page was left intentionally
blank for cutting activity on
previous page.

Invite your child to send a note to someone special using the notepaper below. Encourage your child to draw and color a special picture in the space provided. If interested, he or she might also like to "write" the special person's name on the lines. Then let your child cut out and fold the note. Use a sticker to seal the flap.

This page was left intentionally
blank for cutting activity on
previous page.

Traditional Manuscript

Practice by tracing the letter. Then write the letter.

A A A A A A A A

a a a a a a a

B B B B B B B

b b b b b b b

Traditional Manuscript

Practice by tracing the letter. Then write the letter.

C C C C C C C

c c c c c c c

D D D D D D D

d d d d d d d

Traditional Manuscript

Practice by tracing the letter. Then write the letter.

Traditional Manuscript

Practice by tracing the letter. Then write the letter.

G G G G G G G

g g g g g g g

H H H H H H H

h h h h h h h

Traditional Manuscript

Practice by tracing the letter. Then write the letter.

Summer Link Super Edition Grade K

Traditional Manuscript

Practice by tracing the letter. Then write the letter.

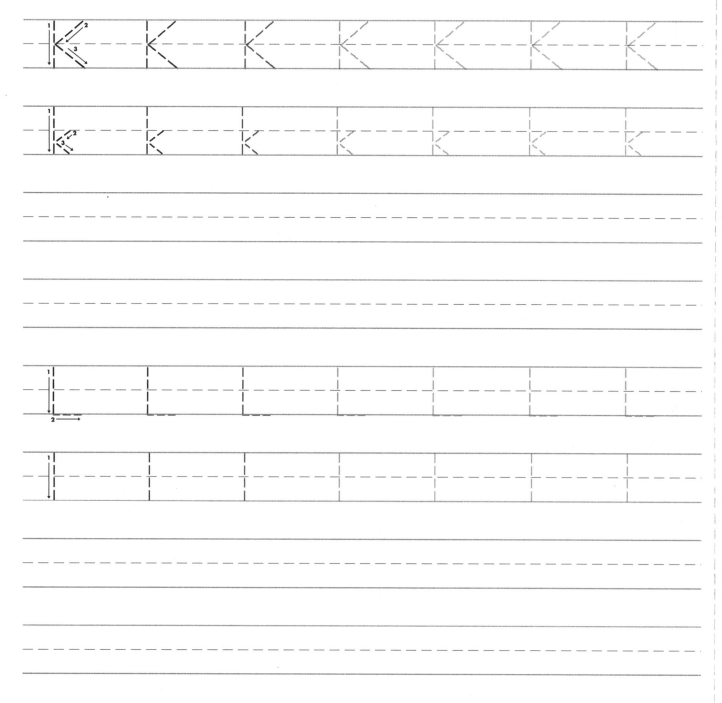

Traditional Manuscript

Practice by tracing the letter. Then write the letter.

M M M M M M M M

m m m m m m m m

N N N N N N N N

n n n n n n n n

Traditional Manuscript

Practice by tracing the letter. Then write the letter.

O O O O O O O

O O O O O O O

P P P P P P P

P P P P P P P

Traditional Manuscript

Practice by tracing the letter. Then write the letter.

Q Q Q Q Q Q Q

q q q q q q q

R R R R R R R

r r r r r r r

Traditional Manuscript

Practice by tracing the letter. Then write the letter.

Traditional Manuscript

Practice by tracing the letter. Then write the letter.

U U U U U U U

U U U U U U U

V V V V V V V

V V V V V V V

Traditional Manuscript

Practice by tracing the letter. Then write the letter.

Traditional Manuscript

Practice by tracing the letter. Then write the letter.

Summer Link Super Edition Grade K

Parent Notes

Parent Notes

Name _____

Parent Notes